REACTIONS TO GOD

REACTIONS TO GOD

Man's Response to God's Activity
in the Psalms

by

Leonard Griffith

HODDER AND STOUGHTON
LONDON   SYDNEY   AUCKLAND   TORONTO

Dedicated to

MERELIE

who has shown me that

*"Many waters cannot quench love,
neither can the floods drown it . . ."*

British Library Cataloguing in Publication Data

Griffith, Leonard
    Reactions to God.
    1. Bible. Old Testament. Psalms—Commentaries
    I. Title
    223′ .2′06   BS1430.3

ISBN 0 340 23600 0

First published 1979

Phototypeset in V.I.P. Baskerville by
Western Printing Services Ltd, Bristol
Printed in Great Britain for
Hodder and Stoughton Ltd.,
Mill Road, Dunton Green, Sevenoaks, Kent
by Lowe & Brydone Printers Ltd., Thetford, Norfolk

Contents

Introduction

This book is a sequel to my earlier volume, *God in Man's Experience, The Activity of God in the Psalms.*[1] I introduced that book by sharing with the reader what the Psalms have meant to me in my personal devotions over the years, how they have helped me to pray and become my means of approach to the presence of God. Through the rest of the Bible God speaks to man, but through the Psalms man speaks to God.

Not only so, but he speaks in a universal language. Every person can find himself somewhere in the Old Testament Psalter. There is at least one Hebrew poet who identifies with him, whose situation mirrors his own and who therefore can take him by the hand and lead him into the presence of God.

To the Psalmists God was a real character in the drama of human life. They consciously brought him into their experience and found that he did for them what no one else could do. Indeed, no collection of writings in the world so completely covers the whole range of God's activity in man's experience. Each Psalm tells its own story—of how the author turned to God and experienced him in a particular way. One found him to be the God who cares, another the God who pardons, another the God who heartens or supports or pursues. It was when I studied the Psalter with that theme in mind and realised that God can be to us now what he once was to the Hebrew poets that I felt impelled to write *God in Man's Experience*.

The acceptance of that book has been surprising and gratifying. Even now, ten years after its publication, I still receive letters from people in many parts of the world telling what it has contributed to their appreciation of the Psalms and to the deepening of their devotional life. Of all the books I have written, it is the one that seems most effectively to exercise a Christian ministry. It is the book that people have given to their friends to help them through personal crises and periods of spiritual drought. It is the book that they have kept on the bedside table to read first thing in the morning or last thing at night. More than one reader has kindly suggested that a companion volume on the Psalms would be welcome.

For a time I actually considered developing the same theme in the experience of a different group of Psalmists. I did look at a different group but realised that to fit them into the old theme would be to tell only half their story. These Old Testament writers record not only how God acted in their experience but how *they reacted* to the activity of God. They tell not only what God did for them but how they responded to God's grace and power. Thus a new theme emerged with fascination and challenge, a theme that brings the Psalms even closer to our lives.

Again I went carefully through the Psalter, this time to study not only God's activity but our human response to that activity. At once I was struck by the variety of response, the variety of moods and the boldness of the Psalmists to express them. They feel happy and depressed, secure and temporary, unworthy, cheated, envious and proud. Each author tells exactly how he feels. He expresses our feelings in the presence of God, and in that sense we can identify with him even more deeply.

So that is the theme of this new book which I offer with the hope that it will provide the reader with a new key to the treasure-house of human devotion and bind him more closely to God. I acknowledge a debt to numerous commentaries, though my expositions are based less upon their use than upon the use of the Psalms in my own devotional life.

I thank Mrs. Maureen Corbett who prepared the manuscript; and Mrs. Muriel Allen who read the proofs. In my treatment of Psalms 73 and 104 I gratefully acknowledge permission from Hodder and Stoughton and from the Lutterworth Press to follow outlines of thought similar to those used in my earlier titles. Except where otherwise indicated, I have followed the text of the Authorised Version of the Bible.

Leonard Griffith

Toronto, Canada, 1978

1. Published by Hodder and Stoughton, London, 1968.

Psalm 8

He Feels Great

"When I consider thy Heavens . . ." What happens when we consider the heavens? Some people never consider the heavens; they never consider very much above eye-level. As far as they are concerned, the heavens are there, that's all, and unless they come tumbling down, why bother about them? Suppose we do consider the heavens, look at them, study them, search them and consider their place in the total scheme of things. What happens then?

One possibility is that we end up feeling rather small, smaller than a grain of sand on the ocean floor. The mind staggers at the sheer size of the heavens. On a clear night the stars seem close enough to touch, yet astronomers tell us that they are unbelievably far away; in fact, so far that their light, which travels at 186,000 miles per second, takes hundreds of years to reach us. And there are so many millions of stars; they cover the heavens like a snowstorm in reverse. Even God, surely, would not miss a little star, like the one on which we live, if suddenly it passed out of the picture. That's one reaction when we consider the heavens.

Then there is the reaction of the person who wrote the 8th Psalm. He also considered the heavens. In fact, he probably thought about them more often and more deeply than we do, because they were the roof under which he worked. Tradition assumes that he was King David, a poet and musician, and that this was one of the Psalms that he composed when he was a young man taking care of his father's sheep on the hills near Bethlehem. When he knew that the animals were bedded down for the night he would lie on his back and look up at the heavens before falling asleep. He saw them as God's heavens, the work of God's fingers. They spoke to him of the glory of God and they didn't make him feel small; on the contrary, they made him feel rather great. He poured out his feelings in a prayer: *"When I consider thy heavens, the work of thy fingers, the moon and the stars, which thou hast ordained; What is man, that thou art mindful of him? and the son of man, that thou visitest him? For thou hast made him a little lower than the angels, and hast crowned him with glory and honour. Thou madest him to have dominion over the works of thy hands; thou hast put all things under his feet . . ."*

There was an old preacher in New England who caught the spirit of the 8th Psalm. Every year he preached a sermon to his rural congregation on the latest discoveries in astronomy. When someone asked what use such a sermon could have in such a place, he replied, "None at all, but it greatly enlarges my idea of God." Astronomy did that for the Psalmist and something else besides. It enlarged not only his idea of God but also his idea of man. It gave him a sense of his own greatness—not the false greatness which assumes equality with God, but man's true greatness in the whole scheme of God's creation. Our generation needs to recover some of the tremendous truths about man that came to the Psalmist as he considered the heavens.

One truth is that *man is God's special concern.* "What is man, that thou art mindful of him . . .?" To be mindful of a person means to think about him, care for him, consider him and have his interests at heart. A loving father is mindful of his children. In his attitudes, his conversation, his conduct and in his demands of life he will do nothing that causes his children to suffer. He will sacrifice his own pleasures for their sake. He makes no decisions without taking them into account. It was a typical father who refused an attractive job offer in another city, because it came at a crucial time in the education of his children, and he didn't want to uproot them. He was mindful of them.

The Bible asks us to believe the same about God. Though he holds the stars in their courses and presides over his vast universe, yet he is mindful of the very least of his human creatures. They are his special concern, more precious to him than all the glittering galaxies in heaven above. That may be difficult to believe when we consider the heavens, but we should look very silly saying our prayers if we didn't believe it. We go to God because we believe that he is concerned more about worth than about size. We believe, as Jesus said, that God is prepared to let the whole universe run itself while he attends to the needs of one human soul. Every church spire that pokes its head above the office buildings, every congregation that sings "Praise God from whom all blessings flow", every child who prays "Now I lay me down to sleep", testifies to God's special concern for his human children. "What is man, that thou art mindful of him . . .?"

". . . and the son of man, that thou visitest him?" Modern Bibles change that to read "care for him". Yet there is truth in the old translation, and it comes very close to the truth of the Gospel. The father of John the Baptist blessed the Lord God of Israel, "for he hath visited and redeemed his people". (Luke 1:68 AV) In Jesus Christ, God visited the human race, came to stay with us, made our home his home, our life his life. He may have visited other planets in his vast universe, but we don't know about them. We do know that he visited our planet and became, as the prophets foretold, "Emmanuel . . . God with us", God beside us, among us and for us. (Matt 1:23 AV) He showed that we are his special concern.

The Psalmist, who lived hundreds of years before Christ, could not share that insight or even perceive its possibility. Yet he did perceive the hand of God in human affairs, the presence of God in human experience, the role of God in human history. He did have the spiritual insight to know that man is infinitely precious to God, so precious that God does for him what he does not do for any of the planets and solar systems: he is mindful of him and visits him, he loves him with an everlasting love.

Another truth that came to the Psalmist as he considered the heavens is that *man is God's highest creation*. "For thou hast made him a little lower than the angels . . .". The Epistle to the Hebrews suggests that man may be higher than the angels. In a passage commonly read on Christmas Day the New Testament writer asks, "For to what angel did God ever say, 'Thou art my Son, today I have begotten thee'? Or again, 'I will be to him a father, and he shall be to me a son'?'' (Heb 1:5 RSV). That accords with a later translation of the Psalm which does not say that man is a little lower than the angels but that man is "little less than God". (RSV)

However we translate the Old Testament poet, he must have soaked his mind in the first chapter of the Book of Genesis. He believed that man, created in God's image, differs from all other creatures not only in degree but in kind. His affinity is with the Maker, not with the made. He has reason, intelligence, the faculty of creating and appreciating beauty, the ability to distinguish between right and wrong and the freedom to choose right or wrong. Man is like God. He has eternal personality. He can think God's thoughts after him and rejoice in that in which God rejoices. The stars in their courses are wonderful, and astronomy opens up the greatness of the universe, but greater than astronomy is the astronomer. In fact, the greatest of all wonders, short of God, is the mind of man.

To a cynic that may sound like colossal conceit. He would dismiss the Psalmist as the child of a pre-scientific age which naively assumed that man was the centre of the universe and that the universe revolved around him. Yet in a moral and spiritual sense was that so very naive? If the Psalmist were alive today, and if we brought him up to date on modern scientific theories, he might change the form but not the substance of his thought. He would still see human personality as the crown and flower of the cosmic universe. He would still think of man as God's highest creation. He might look at the heavens through a telescope instead of with the naked eye and perhaps pick out a man-made satellite cruising among the stars but would still challenge the astronomers and the astronauts to find a higher and more marvellous creation than the human soul. He might even quote Tennyson, a comparatively modern poet, who wrote,

> Though world on world in myriad myriads roll
>   Round us, each with different powers,
>   And other forms of life than ours,
> What know we greater than the soul?

There are two more truths that came to the Psalmist as he

considered the heavens, and each truth interprets the other. The first is that *man is God's most honoured creature*. "For thou hast made him a little lower than the angels, and hast crowned him with glory and honour." Those are words normally reserved for kings. They denote a royal status and by themselves scarcely seem applicable to ordinary people. They make sense, however, in the light of the second truth which declares that *man is God's deputy in the world*. He is king by virtue of the lordship which God has given him over all creation. *"Thou madest him to have dominion over the works of thy hands; thou hast put all things under his feet: All sheep and oxen, yea, and the beasts of the field; The fowl of the air, and the fish of the sea, and whatsoever passeth through the paths of the seas. O Lord our Lord, how excellent is thy name in all the earth!"*

If the Psalm were written today, the writer would not stop there. He might not even mention sheep and oxen and fowl and fish, because they don't seem so very wonderful any more, except when they are in short supply. He would rejoice in the achievement of Sir Edmund Hilary who stood on the summit of Mount Everest and said afterwards, "I had the world lie beneath my clumsy boots." He would exult in man's dominion over the forces of nature, his splitting of the atom and harnessing the sun's rays and making the ether waves his messengers. The Old Testament poet spoke in a much larger sense than he realised.

Imagine his amazement if someone from the twentieth century could travel back through time and sit beside him under the night sky on the Judean hills. We might say to him, "Can you believe that the moon up there, which fills you with wonder and seems so close, is actually 250,000 miles away? That's the journey from Dan to Beersheba 2500 times. And would you believe it if we tell you that some day a person is going to travel that distance through space and put his clumsy boots on the moon's surface? Not only so, but when he is up there he is going to hold a conversation with people here on earth. Think of that next time you say to God, 'Thou hast put all things under his feet'." Chances are that the Psalmist would not believe us. If he did believe us he would probably reply, "God has crowned man with a greater glory, a greater honour than I could ever have dreamed. Man is certainly God's most honoured creature!"

Some ecologists would dispute that. They do not appreciate

the 8th Psalm. They insist that the Hebrew poet led man astray when he said that God created him to have dominion over the earth and all its creatures. They blame the religion of the Psalm for giving man the wrong idea that God created this world solely for his benefit and that he is free to dominate and exploit it for his own use. They hold the Psalmist and other Bible writers responsible for all the problems of pollution, erosion, famine and over-population that threaten to make the earth uninhabitable. Paul Ehrlich in his apocalyptic book, *The Population Bomb*, points out that, if we hope to solve our ecological problems, we have to change from a growth-oriented, exploitative system to one that focuses on stability and conservation. That means that our whole attitude toward nature must undergo a revolution. "That revolution", writes Dr. Ehrlich, "is going to be extremely difficult to pull off, since the attitudes of Western culture are deeply rooted in the Judaeo-Christian tradition. Unlike people in many other cultures, we see man's basic role as that of dominating nature rather than living in harmony with it."[1]

It is possible that Dr. Ehrlich has not really studied the Judaeo-Christian tradition in the Bible, else he might realise that God does intend us to live in harmony with nature. God has made us the trustees of his world and has given us a sacred obligation to preserve and care for it. Christians agree with the ecologists but they express their convictions differently. They believe that the problem lies not in God's mandate but in man's sinful nature. Although he has mastered his environment, he has not yet mastered himself. He has solved some of the problems of physical nature but not the problems of his own human nature. He controls the beasts of the field but not the beasts in his own heart, the beasts of pride and greed and selfishness that make him suffer and cause innocent people to suffer, that put him at odds with his environment and fracture his friendship with God. Man will never exercise his rightful lordship over creation until he subjects himself to the Lordship of the Creator. When he falls below that he drags the whole creation down with him, and creation will be redeemed only when man himself is redeemed.

That is beyond the scope of the Psalm, but not beyond the scope of the Judaeo-Christian tradition in the Bible. In fact, the real difference between that tradition and others lies in its insistence that man cannot solve his human problems, he cannot save himself, he needs help from beyond. Christians believe that God sent that help in Jesus Christ. They believe that in the life, death and resurrection of Christ God has acted to redeem man and therefore to redeem the whole creation. In that very act of redemption he has crowned man with glory and honour and given him his royal status.

Here, then, is one of the earliest Psalms in the Old Testament pointing to its fulfilment in the New Testament. In fact, one New Testament writer quotes the Psalmist's words, "Thou hast crowned him with glory and honour, putting everything in subjection under his feet." This writer can see that man, because of sin, does not rightfully exercise his lordship over all creation. "As it is, we do not yet see everything in subjection to him." From the Christian perspective, however, the writer can see something else. He adds, "But we see Jesus, who for a little while was made lower than the angels, crowned with glory and honour . . ." (Heb 2:7-9 RSV).

Jesus is the Man par excellence, the Representative Man, the Pattern Man, the measure and stature of manhood as God created it without sin. God crowned him with glory and honour and in so doing gave a royal status to the whole human race. The human race produced Jesus. He did not come down from the heavens. He came up from the earth. He was bone of our bone and flesh of our flesh, the son of a peasant maiden who was married to a village carpenter, a descendant of the writer of the 8th Psalm. The human race *could* produce Jesus. It had the potential to produce Jesus. God placed the royal crown on man's head when he made him potentially Christlike. In his relation to Christ man is truly great, and in his relation to Christ every person may decide his own greatness.

NOTES TO PSALM 8

1. Paul Ehrlich, *The Population Bomb*, Ballentine Books, New York, 1968, p. 170.

Psalm 11

He Feels Resolved

The writer of the 11th Psalm responds to God with a question and with an answer. He asks, *"If the foundations are destroyed, what can the righteous do?"*[1] That is a very real question today, simply because all kinds of foundations are being destroyed, especially the moral foundations on which some of us have based our lives and on which our civilisation has been built.

After the Second World War, Elton Trueblood wrote a short but significant book about the Ten Commandments called *Foundations for Reconstruction*.[2] At that time statesmen were, in fact, trying to reconstruct our shattered world and were seeking foundations on which to build. Trueblood pointed out that they did not have to look far, because God gave those foundations to the human race thirty centuries ago: "Thou shalt have no other gods before me . . . Honour thy father and thy mother . . . Thou shalt not steal . . . Thou shalt not kill . . . Thou shalt not covet. . ." Said Trueblood, Let us rebuild our post-war world on the firm God-given foundation of the Ten Commandments, and it will be a world where people can live together securely, happily and nobly.

Yet those are the very foundations that are being destroyed. On a single day a single issue of a Toronto newspaper carried three items.[3] The first quoted a Cabinet Minister who disappointed many Canadians by saying in the House of Commons, "If I cannot impose my morality on adults in the bedrooms of Canada, I do not see how I can go to another country and judge their morality." The second was "An Open Letter of Concern" signed by a Roman Catholic Archbishop pleading with people to protest the rising cesspool of pornographic literature and to pray for moral decency in our society. The third concerned a doctor who was exonerated after performing more than six hundred illegal abortions and has become something of a public hero, receiving more than $50,000 from supporters across Canada to help pay his legal fees. Before wrapping the garbage in that particular page of the newspaper I wrote across the top, "If the foundations are destroyed, what can the righteous do?"

The easiest and most obvious answer is "Nothing!" In fact, the safest thing to do, when a building starts to collapse, is to get out and as far away as possible. The Psalmist, who was a righteous man, toyed with that idea—*"flee like a bird to the mountains"*. That is the reaction of many righteous people today. We all have our emotional mountains to which we can flee and from which we can watch the world going to hell—mountains of neutrality, inactivity, resignation, self-righteousness and disgust. Yet that is a cowardly reaction, and the Psalmist did not entertain it for very long. He looked at the world in the light of his religious faith and answered his own question. He resolved that, if the foundations are destroyed, there are some very definite things that the righteous can do.

The righteous can still believe in God. The Psalmist must have been speaking to his own cowardly self when he began the Psalm by saying, *"In the Lord I take refuge; how can you say to me, 'flee like a bird to the mountains'?"* He was saying, in effect, "Why should I flee? God has not fled. He is still sovereign . . . *The Lord is in his holy temple, the Lord's throne is in heaven.*"

The late Halford Luccock told of a priceless printer's error that appeared in the programme of a performance of Handel's Messiah. It listed the Hallelujah Chorus as follows, "The Lord God Omnipotent *resigneth*". Dr. Luccock went on to ask, "Was it really an error, or was the printer a cynic, deducing from the condition of the world that the Lord God had resigned or that he was about to give the world up as a hopeless mess?"

It seems that way at times in spite of what Scripture says. From cover to cover the Bible confronts us with the stirring truth of God's sovereignty. It presents a God who, having created the world, controls and governs the world and involves himself in its affairs; a God who, having started history in motion, presides over history and directs it according to his wise and good purpose; a God who, having ordained moral laws for the well-being of his creatures, administers those laws and judges us according to them. The Bible declares that, no matter what is happening in the world, God knows all about it and has the situation in hand. Yet that belief comes very hard these days. How shall we express faith in God's sovereignty at a time when the world looks like a mental hospital where the guards are on strike and the patients have seized control?

We shall express our faith in many different ways, one in particular. We shall identify with the community of faith because we know that we can never go it alone. What can the righteous do? They can find strengthening fellowship with other righteous, those who stand week by week in the presence of God and say their prayers and recite the historic creeds and read the Bible and hear its message applied to modern life. In the Lord we do take refuge when we go to church—not as a means of escape from reality but as a means of seeing reality in its eternal perspective, a means of dwelling for a time in the eternal world of which this passing world is only a pale shadow.

A minister once said in a sermon, "My friends, we are living in two worlds." He was challenged afterwards by a businessman who asked, "Did you really mean that about living in two worlds?" The minister repeated his conviction. "If I could believe that," said the businessman, "I should change every major business decision before midnight." The point is that we *are* living in two worlds. We are living in a man's world where the foundations which have supported our lives for centuries are now being destroyed. We are living in God's world where the foundations are eternal and cannot be destroyed. Thus God declared through a New Testament writer: "Yet once more I shake not the earth only but also heaven . . . signifying the removing of those things that are shaken . . . that those things which cannot be shaken may remain" (Heb 12:26, 27 AV).

Augustine saw that truth in the fourth century. When the barbarian hordes were attacking Rome, he sat down in that hour of darkness and despair and wrote a book which has since become a classic of Christian literature. He called it *Concerning the City of God*, and this, in effect, is what he said to his readers:

You thought that the passing of Rome and the stability
which she gave to the world meant the end of
everything from the point of view of the church. You
were utterly wrong. Rome was an earthly city and shall
not be everlasting. The church is divine, and therefore
indestructible. Human cities may rise and fall, but the
City of God remains . . .

"If the foundations are destroyed, what can the righteous
do?" Like the Psalmist they can resolve to go on believing in
God.

They can also keep on being righteous. They can do their own thing
in a world that does everything else. They can continue to
pursue simple goodness. They can keep the inner citadel of the
soul clean and wholesome in the sight of him whose *"eyes behold
. . . the children of men"*, who *"tests the righteous and the wicked, and
his soul hates him that loves violence"*.

After reading those depressing newspaper items I wrote my
own item, an article pleading for the revival of some basic
virtues in our society.[4] Although some people don't like the
word "revival", even when applied to religion, I insisted that
there are times when progress points backwards, and one of
those times could be right now. Instead of trying to create new
moral standards we need to recover some of the old ones that we
have lost. The article specified eight virtues.

1. *Honesty*: If society were not basically honest, we should be
living in a jungle. There is, however, an alarming amount of
peripheral dishonesty which we have learned to live with like a
low-grade infection and which needs to be exposed and cured.

2. *Integrity*: The word comes from "integrated" which
means 'united, all of a piece, the same inside and out". What
troubled Canadians about the Cabinet Minister's statement
was the implication that our moral behaviour need not be the
same inside and outside the country. It suggested that dishonesty in business is acceptable as long as we don't commit it at
home.

3. *Decency*: The Archbishop did not call pornography a sin.
He called it indecent, and that's what it is. The subject matter
of many magazines, books, movies, plays and television pro-

grammes is moral garbage. It pollutes human minds, especially the minds of young people, and needs to be cleaned up.

4. *Industry*: That means hard work. It used to be a way of life in the democracies until some people began bargaining with it and others decided that it was just as profitable not to work. Profitable to them, perhaps, but not to society as a whole.

5. *Frugality*: That's not being poor but living within our means, and doing so not by compulsion but by choice. The reason for it is to identify with the human race, half of whom are poor, sick, hungry and ignorant. We cannot continue to inhabit a paradise of ease suspended in a hell of global insecurity.

6. *Courtesy*: There is too much rudeness in our society, and it carries people to ugly and violent extremes. It causes highway accidents, labour disputes, racial incidents and marriage breakdowns. Courtesy costs nothing to practise but it yields high dividends in sweeter human relationships.

7. *Loyalty*: Many people today have no loyalties. They are not bad people but they care only for themselves and feel no obligation, no strong sense of allegiance to anyone or anything bigger than themselves. They are prepared to desert their country, their employers, their families and their friends in order to grasp the happiness which they believe that life owes them. A feature of moral revival would be a reawakening of loyalty in all areas of life.

8. *Charity*: That is a sturdy virtue which goes far beyond making an annual donation to organised philanthropy. Charity is not a "Great White Father" complex but an attitude of caring concern, especially toward those who are older and weaker and less privileged. It is at the very heart of justice and social responsibility.

Those are the common virtues, the moral foundations of society which today are being destroyed. You can see them being destroyed every time you watch television or pick up a newspaper. What can the righteous do? At the very least they can keep on being righteous, keep on practising those old-fashioned virtues even in a society where they are not generally practised. The righteous person can still file an honest income-tax return. He can still be a person whose private and public personalities are the same. He can still refuse to read salacious literature or attend gutter movies. He can still give a fair day's work for a fair day's pay. He can still practise self-denial. He can still be polite to people wherever he meets them and whoever they are. He can still be true to those who trust him. He can still help a neighbour in need. God gave those virtues to the human race, he made them visible in the character of Christ, he gives us the incentive and the courage to practise them now. "If the foundations are destroyed, what can the righteous do?" Like the Psalmist they can resolve to keep on being righteous.

They can also maintain a sense of Divine companionship. The last verse reads, "*The Lord is righteous, he loves righteous deeds; the upright shall behold his face.*" That recalls a passage from the Book of Revelation where the inspired writer describes the heavenly city, New Jerusalem, the city of righteous deeds and righteous thoughts. He says, "The throne of God and of the Lamb shall be in it, and his servants shall worship him; they shall see his face, and his name shall be on their foreheads" (22:3, 4 RSV). What a comforting assurance about those whom we have loved and lost, and what a glorious hope for ourselves—to be in the presence of God eternally and see his face! The Psalmist, however, does not defer that hope to eternity. When he uses the phrase, "the upright shall behold his face", he means that here and now we can be in God's presence and enjoy fellowship with him.

When the foundations are destroyed, it makes a tremendous difference to be with someone whom you love and trust. In a working-class area of South London there is a remarkable institution, sponsored by the Methodist Church, called Clubland that ministers entirely to adolescent boys on a seven-day-a-week basis. It serves them meals, provides them with athletic facilities, hobby shops, cultural courses, and has a beautiful chapel at the centre of its life. Its redemptive and character-building influence in that unfavourable environment is too great to be measured. Clubland was bombed during the Second World War. Standing out on the street and surveying the ruins, the director threw up his hands in despair and cried, "This is the end! I have lost everything." One of the lads retorted, "No you ain't. You've still got us." He did have them. He had their loyalty and their love which saw him through the crisis and inspired him to rebuild Clubland as it is today.

To behold the face of God means to know that, when the foundations are destroyed, we've still got the love and loyalty of God. We *can* behold his face because we have seen his glory in the face of Jesus Christ. *He* is the God to whom we have access, who offers us his friendship and invites us to walk beside him. As long as we have that God we can never say that we have lost everything. We can always rebuild.

That was Martin Luther King's experience in one of the worst crises of his life. In the middle of the night he was awakened by the telephone. An angry voice said, "Listen, nigger, we've taken all we want from you. Before next week you'll be sorry you ever came to this town." It was just another of the many abusive calls, and Martin felt he could take it no longer. He went into the kitchen and made himself a cup of coffee and began to think calmly of the position he was in and what the alternatives were. At last he bowed over the table and prayed aloud saying, "Lord, I am taking a stand for what I believe is right. The people are looking to me for leadership, and if I stand before them without strength and courage, they will falter. I am at the end of my power. I have nothing left. I have come to the point where I can't face it alone." Later he said to his wife, "At that moment I experienced the presence of the Divine as I had never experienced him before. It seemed as though I could hear the quiet assurance of an inner voice saying, 'Stand up for righteousness, stand up for truth; and God will be at your side forever'."[5]

"If the foundations are destroyed, what can the righteous do?" Like the writer of the 11th Psalm they can resolve to believe in God, to keep on being righteous and to maintain a sense of Divine companionship. That's what they can do.

NOTES TO PSALM 11

1. The treatment of this Psalm follows the translation in the Revised Standard Version.
2. Published by Harper & Row, New York, 1946.
3. *The Globe and Mail*, 2 December 1976.
4. Published in the *Toronto Sunday Sun*, 26 December, 1976.
5. From *My Life With Martin Luther King, Jr.* by Coretta Scott King. Published 1969 by Hodder and Stoughton Ltd.

Psalm 19

He Feels Warned

A motorist, driving along a city street from east to west, comes to a busy intersection where the traffic light turns green. He continues driving, knowing that the north and southbound traffic have a red light and must stop. He is protected by the law. At the next corner he stops at a red light, because if he keeps on driving, the law will not protect but condemn him. As he approaches the third intersection the light flashes yellow, as it usually does in Canadian cities. Now he has a split-second choice either to accelerate or slow down and stop. If he is wise he will apply the brakes. Now the law is warning him.

Those are three functions of the law — to protect, to condemn and to warn. Often the law acts on people like a yellow traffic light, deterring them from conduct which is criminal or dangerous or anti-social. The law warns them, and they are grateful for the warning. They realise that a society without laws would be like a busy street corner without traffic lights — a scene of confusion and chaos. The laws are there for our good. They are essential to a well-ordered society.

The writer of the 19th Psalm saw the whole universe as a well-ordered society. He believed that when the Father God created it he wrote into its structure certain natural and moral laws for the well-being of his children. Those laws serve the same purpose as the laws of the land: they protect, they condemn and they warn. They warned the Psalmist. He said, "*By them is thy servant warned*." That was his reaction to the laws of God. It's an old-fashioned reaction in these days when people rebel against any kind of moral authority, especially the authority of religion, but it could contain the secret of a quality of life which we are in danger of losing. Examine the Psalmist's thought more closely.

First, he insists that there is a moral order which declares the glory of God no less than the natural order declares the glory of God. The natural order fills him with wonder and awe, as it fills many people with wonder and awe. They marvel at the beauty, the vastness and the steadfast order of the created universe and at the laws which are the basis of its continued existence. I marvelled at those laws when I visited the Manned Spacecraft Centre in Houston, Texas, and saw an astronaut walking on a wall. Suspended by wires at an 18-degree angle, he was training for survival on a planet where his body would be governed by only 7/10ths of the earth's gravity. The presence and dependability of such natural laws as the law of gravity make possible the exploration of outer space and all scientific advance. We did not create those laws. They were here before we came, and we must live within them in order to survive.

Even people who do not normally call themselves religious are willing to believe that nature with its laws declares the glory of God. They may not recognise God in the Bible or the church or the Sacrament or in personal piety but they share the reaction of the Psalmist who said, *"The heavens declare the glory of God; and the firmament sheweth his handywork. Day unto day uttereth speech, and night unto night sheweth knowledge. There is no speech nor language, where their voice is not heard."* If ever there was a statement of universal religion—there it is. Above the confusion of conflicting cultures and civilisations nature speaks to man its universal language and it speaks to him of God. What matter if the Psalmist went on to imply that the sun revolves around the earth rather than the earth around the sun? At least he gave honour to the sun, knowing that the earth's life depends upon it. We can be sure that if he had known all that astronomy now knows he would not have altered a single line but would only have given greater glory to God.

Actually two things filled the Psalmist with wonder and awe. Alongside the natural order he saw a moral order governed by laws which to him seemed just as marvellous as the laws of nature. They also declared the glory of God. His reverent spirit

was shared by the German philosopher, Emmanuel Kant, who
said that two things filled him with wonder and awe—"the
starry heavens above . . . and the moral law within". The
Psalmist might be referring specifically to the Jewish religious
law as it evolved from the Ten Commandments—in which
case we can enlarge his thought to include the moral teachings
of all great religions, supremely the teachings of Jesus. Yet the
Psalmist has something more basic in mind. Linked to the
opening verses, his words suggest that he is extolling not our
human moralities but the very laws that God wrote into the
constitution of the universe when he created it. We could call
them God's ground rules.

God told Adam and Eve what they were. When he placed the
parents of the human race in the Garden of Eden he said, "You
may freely eat of every tree of the garden; but of the tree of the
knowledge of good and evil you shall not eat. . ." (Gen 2:16, 17
RSV). Then along came the snake, who might have been a
moral philosopher, and tempted the woman, saying in effect,
"The trouble with God is that he doesn't want you to know as
much as he knows. He doesn't want you to grow up. There are
no ground rules except those that you make for yourself. *You*
decide what is good and evil." Adam and Eve decided, but they
had to work out their decision on the other side of the garden
fence where there were no fruit trees, only hard ground that had
to be ploughed. Some people call that a quaint story, even a
myth, and they remind us that all civilisations have produced
their creation myths to explain the origin of the world and the
origin of good and evil. They forget that myth is a mighty
vehicle of truth; and the truth of Genesis is the truth echoed
by the 19th Psalm, viz., that there are ground rules, God made
them, they declare his glory, and we have to live within them
in order to survive.

The second major truth to emerge from the 19th Psalm is
that the moral laws, written into the constitution of the universe, are designed for the well-being of God's children. They
are not tyrannical laws that crib and confine but beneficent
laws that release and redeem. God put them there for our good,
and we are happier if we live by them. The Psalmist now
develops that theme in poetic style as he calls the law by its

various names, each time praising it both for its own qualities and for its results.

"The law of the Lord is perfect, converting the soul . . .", i.e., reviving the soul, giving fresh life to a person's inner self. That is a fact of human experience, though not generally recognised. People assume that the unrestricted life is the satisfying life, whereas experience proves that satisfaction is found within the right kind of authority. Young people are quick to remind us of that fact. An American magazine, *U.S. News and World Report*, published an article (July 18, 1977) entitled, "America's Youth: Angry . . . Bored . . . or Just Confused?" which reflected the illusion of permissiveness and which brought a flood of letters from youthful readers. One of them wrote, "A lot of problem youths need militarylike treatment with some religion thrown in. There is too much permissiveness from parents who read books by psychologists who have raised their kids in less-than-typical environments." He adds, "I will say that the article was informative from the 'experts' point of view. Next time, why don't you ask us?"[1]

". . . the testimony of the Lord is sure, making wise the simple". Every person ought to be sure of something. Especially as he grows older he should have at least one unchanging reality to which he can cling in a changing world. For the Psalmist that reality was the law of God. He felt that it made him sure-footed and therefore wise, while people who argued about relative moralities stumbled all over the place. The testimony of the Lord does make wise the simple. Even a child who knows the law of God has a light in the darkness, a compass in the desert, a sure source of wisdom and guidance that will never fail him throughout his life.

"The statutes of the Lord are right, rejoicing the heart . . ." Because they are right they produce in the heart a joy that springs from the inner sense of being in the right. That's not the same as being self-righteous, which can produce the very opposite of joy. Some of the most miserable people in the world are those who believe that they are always right and everybody else is wrong. The Psalmist is talking here about the emotional release, the sense of joy that floods the heart of a person who sees the law of God and obeys it and knows that he has done the right thing. It was the joy of a man who resigned a highly-paid

job because he could not connive at dishonest business practices. When a friend asked how he was getting along, he said, "Fine! I believe that I did the right thing and I am happy, happier than I have ever been before."

". . . *the commandment of the Lord is pure, enlightening the eyes*". It enlightens the eyes to look upon anything that is pure, because once you have seen the real thing you will always recognise an impure product. That applies to precious metals and to precious moral standards. Having seen that the commandment of the Lord is pure, you are not going to be fooled when you see it mixed up with human alloys. You will know that murder is still murder and that adultery is still adultery even when they are excused on the grounds of irresistible impulse and meaningful relationship. You will know that whatever destroys human personality is everlastingly wrong and that whatever elevates human personality is everlastingly right.

"*The fear of the Lord is clean, enduring for ever . . .*" Because respect for the law of God is clean it does endure when systems of permissiveness collapse. In the long experimenting with the sex relationship a single behaviour pattern continually rises to the top as a requisite of human well-being and happiness—the pattern of a man and a woman loving each other so much that they do not care to love anybody else in the same way, building a permanent home that puts around the children the strong security of unbroken affection. That is the arrangement prescribed by the law of God. It is a clean arrangement, enduring forever.

". . . *the judgments of the Lord are true and righteous altogether.*" That is followed by a verse which could relate to it or to all the preceding verses: "*More to be desired are they than gold, yea, than much fine gold: sweeter also than honey and the honeycomb.*" Those are important commodities. If you've got honey and gold you've got just about everything that you could possibly need or want in this life. Gold symbolises the necessities and the power to purchase them. Honey symbolises the luxuries, the delicate satisfactions. But what good are honey and gold without the freedom to acquire them and the liberty to enjoy them? God gives that freedom and that liberty in a world governed by the laws, testimonies, statutes, commandments and judgments which he has designed for the well-being of his children. Those are sweeter than honey and more to be desired than gold.

The third truth that emerges from the 19th Psalm tells how its author reacts to the moral laws which declare God's glory and promote human well-being. He says, *"Moreover by them is thy servant warned . . ."* He sees the law as a yellow traffic light. Presumably, as a man with human weaknesses, he had sometimes gone through the red light and felt condemned by the law. Much of the time the law had protected him as a green traffic light protects pedestrians and drivers. Basically, however, he feels warned by the laws of God and he adds, *"in keeping of them there is great reward."*

He might have added, "In breaking them there is great penalty." To be sure, the laws of God warn but they also contain their own consequences for those who pay no attention to them. They are like the warning that appears on the television screen before movies that exploit sex and violence: "Parental discretion is advised", meaning, "Put the children to bed". It appeared before a picture called "Dirty Harry", the story of a police detective who was always given dirty jobs to do, including shooting it out with a psychotic killer. Some parents did not heed the warning. In Columbus, Ohio, a 14-year-old boy took his 11-year-old brother into their mother's bedroom where they re-enacted scenes from the movie. The younger boy had a toy pistol, and the older lad got a loaded 22-calibre derringer that belonged to his father. Playing the role of Dirty Harry, he shot and killed his brother.

Will that boy's parents ever forgive themselves for failing to heed the warning? It was written for their good just as the laws of God have been written for our good. Our blunders, mistakes and errors, which have been so costly to ourselves and others, should prove to us that we need such laws. As the Psalmist says, *"Who can understand his errors?"* No mystery is more baffling to any person than the mystery of the sins which he commits unwittingly. "I don't know what made me do it," declared a man who had been unfaithful to his wife. "I have never done anything like that before." Many a criminal has said the same thing when arrested for his first offence. Most of us say it about our moral failures, the evil we do and the good we neglect to do. "Who can understand his errors?" The Psalmist welcomed the law of God that warned him against them.

Also he prayed, *"cleanse thou me from secret faults."* He may have meant the faults hidden from others or the faults hidden from himself, though they amount to the same thing. We generally try to hide from ourselves the sins that we hide or fail to hide from others. We rationalise them, pretend that they don't exist, bury them deep in our subconscious minds. Years later, when they start to fester and send up a painful pus, we pay some psychiatrist to bring them out into the light and help us face up to them. We might have faced up to them in the first place if we had heeded the laws of God. The Psalmist gave thanks for those laws which warned him against his secret faults.

Again he prayed, *"Keep back thy servant also from presumptuous sins: let them not have dominion over me."* Other translations speak of "the sins of self-will", though that's not quite the same. "Presumptuous" derives from the verb "to presume"; and to presume upon God means to treat God, in the words of one army chaplain, "as if he were a bloody fool". It means taking God for granted, accepting his gifts without gratitude, playing fast and loose with his laws. That could be *"the great transgression"* from which the Psalmist prays to be innocent. Certainly it is the great transgression of our society today, a secular society that divorces itself from God and makes its own rules and turns its back on the community of faith, a society without gratitude, without reverence, without humility and without obedience. Jesus spoke about the sin against the Holy Spirit, for which there is no forgiveness, only redemption. The Psalmist welcomed the law of God as a warning against the unforgiveable sin.

In the mood of the Psalmist we meditate on the law of God which declares his glory and promotes human happiness and warns us against sin. His final word is a prayer: *"Let the words of my mouth, and the meditation of my heart, be acceptable in thy sight, O Lord, my strength, and my redeemer."*

NOTES TO PSALM 19

1.   *U.S. News and World Report*, 1 August 1977, p. 49.

Psalm 22

He Feels Forsaken

"*My God, my God, why has thou forsaken me?*" Everybody knows that Jesus spoke those words from the Cross. He must have spoken them. No story-teller would have dared to put them on his lips. They have been called his cry of dereliction. It came at three o'clock in the afternoon when Jesus had been on the Cross for six hours and his life was almost spent. Up to that time, in spite of his extreme agony, he had thought not of himself but of others—his crucifiers, the penitent thief, his mother and the beloved disciple—reaching out to them, caring and praying for them in loving concern. Then at noon a deep darkness descended upon the whole earth, blotting out all human goodness and compassion and love; and out of the darkness came this piercing cry from the Cross, "My God, my God, why hast thou forsaken me?" (Mark 15:34). Everybody knows that Jesus spoke those words.

Not everybody knows that they are the opening words of the 22nd Psalm which has been called the Psalm of the Cross. The author, whatever his name, seems to have been physically ill to the point of death. He vividly pictures his symptoms: "*I am poured out like water, and all my bones are out of joint: my heart is like wax; it is melted in the midst of my bowels. My strength is dried up like a potsherd; and my tongue cleaveth to my jaws . . .*" He could stand his physical pain if it were not for the emotional distress caused by the indifference of God and the mockery of men. "*All they that see me laugh me to scorn; they shoot out the lip, they shake the head saying, He trusted on the Lord that he would deliver him: let him deliver him, seeing he delighted in him.*" The Psalmist compares his foes in their ferocity to strong bulls, ravening and roaring lions, hunters closing in on a wild beast or dragging it off for the kill. They stare and gloat over him as his death draws near. They anticipate his death, dividing his garments among them like looters after an execution. They even hasten his death by piercing his hands and feet. Despised and rejected by men, the poor victim turns to God and suffers the most crushing blow of all. God isn't there. Even God seems to have forsaken him.

Is it any wonder that Jesus, who had known and recited the Psalms since childhood, should have begun to recite this one during his dark hours on the Cross? The Psalmist's experience described him exactly. It was all happening to him. The Scripture says that "he cried out with a loud voice", which means that everyone at Calvary heard his cry of dereliction and everyone except the Roman soldiers knew that he was quoting the 22nd Psalm. He may have intended to quote all of it but could not because his strength was exhausted, his lips stained with blood, his mouth parched with thirst. Yet the fact that he started to say the Psalm suggests that it filled his mind during those three terrible hours of silent darkness. If that is true, if the whole of the 22nd Psalm occupied his thoughts, it provides a new insight into his agony and triumph, a new understanding of his cry from the Cross, "My God, my God, why hast thou forsaken me?" In the light of the 22nd Psalm how do we hear that cry?

We hear it as *an intensely human cry*. We realise that the suffering, the darkness, the loneliness and the God-forsakenness were not an experience peculiar to the Son of God. We can be sure that it must have been especially agonising for him, more agonising than the scourge that tore his back and nails that pierced his hands and feet. All his life he had believed in God's loving concern, and now his faith wavered, not because he was on the Cross but because the Cross was there at all and because his own way of loving concern had brought him there. All his life he had shown people the victory of faith in God; and he was now a passive, helpless victim ending his own life in defeat. All his life he had possessed a sublime sense of the presence of God, and now in the hour of his death God had forsaken him. The wonder of it is not that he uttered his cry of dereliction after being on the Cross for six hours but that he did not utter it much sooner.

Yet the very fact that the cry originated not with him but with a Hebrew Psalmist shows that the experience of feeling forsaken by God is a human experience. We don't know if King David wrote the 22nd Psalm, but it certainly fits him like a glove. He knew the cruel ingratitude and murderous hate which made him a hunted and harried fugitive with a price on his head. He suffered the bitterness of betrayal which drove him to exile. He endured the vitriolic verbal derision of gloating enemies. His trusted friends abandoned him, and there were times when heaven itself seemed indifferent to his harsh and apparently hopeless fate. From the depths of human despair King David could easily have cried out, "My God, my God, why hast thou forsaken me?"

That intensely human cry is as modern as it is ancient. Alan Paton made it the theme of his moving book, *Cry, the Beloved Country*,[1] set in South Africa. It is the story of Kumalo, an old and humble Zulu parson, who came from his native village to Johannesburg, "the city of evil", looking for his sister and his only son. First, he made the terrible discovery that his sister had turned prostitute and bootlegger. Then, after an agonising search, he found his son in prison, charged with the murder of a white man. It was more than his spirit could bear. Crushed, numbed and grief-stricken, he refused to be comforted. He felt alone, forsaken, lost in the stars. "There are times", he said to a missionary friend, "when God seems no more to be about the world."

The Cross of Jesus Christ touched old Kumalo as it touches many people at the point of their God-forsakenness. They are not atheists. They don't say that God has never been there but that God has gone away and left them at the time when they needed him most. All their lives they have believed in him, said their prayers, worshipped him in church and tried to live according to his laws. Yet when they came to their Calvary of suffering, pain, anguish and sorrow, he wasn't there, he didn't meet them in their need. They felt lost in the stars, lost in the darkness where there were no stars. The Cross touches many people at precisely that point.

In doing so, the Cross becomes their link with God, perhaps

their only link. There are many fine, tortured, sensitive souls who thank God that Jesus uttered his cry of dereliction from the Cross, because it brings him down to the very depths of our human experience and makes the Incarnation a complete Incarnation. When I was a minister in Britain I preached a sermon, that was reported in the newspapers, in which I evaluated the Bishop of Woolwich's book, *Honest to God*, and in which I accused the Bishop of not having much faith left. One woman wrote me a tear-stained letter saying that I ought to respect what little faith people have. She told me that she had lost her husband and her father and that she herself was ill with cancer. She said that her only link with God was Jesus' cry from the Cross, "My God, my God, why hast thou forsaken me?", and what right had I to deprecate any link, however tenuous? For her sake and the sake of many others we can only give thanks that the Son of God uttered that cry which is the cry of so many human hearts.

In the context of the 22nd Psalm we hear it also as *a cry of faith*. It must have been that, or the Old Testament writer would have stopped there. Instead, he went on and reminded God of his goodness to past generations. *"Our fathers trusted in thee: they trusted, and thou didst deliver them."* He remembered God's goodness to him in his own childhood. *"But thou art he that took me out of the womb: thou didst make me hope when I was upon my mother's breasts."* He was not about to let this God go.

Nor was Jesus about to let God go. Though he felt abandoned by God on the Cross, he did not dismiss God from the scheme of things but turned to him in prayer, and it was a prayer of stubborn and courageous faith. Even in the darkness of God's absence he still claimed God as his own, still called him *"My* God". In the cry itself he was not berating God, not even reproaching him but reaching out like a child for his Father's hand and saying, "My friends have gone. It is dark. I have great pain and I am alone. Please Father, do not leave me."

Did God leave Jesus, did he really forsake him and give him up? Does God ever forsake his children who love and trust him? In Alan Paton's story old Kumalo received his answer from an English priest. After his son had been found guilty and sentenced to death, he cried out in despair, "It seems that God has turned from me." The priest replied, "That may seem to happen. But it does not happen, never, never does it happen." That's what faith is all about really. Faith is believing that God is never closer to us than in the darkness of our suffering and sin. Faith is believing that God is in the midst of that black, ugly darkness, bringing out all possible good. Faith is believing that God never forsakes us, even though we forsake him. Faith is praying to God even when there seems no one and nothing there. Faith is calling him "*My* God".

Faith is also contending with God, as Jesus contended when he cried out, "*Why* hast thou forsaken me?" Perhaps we have been taught that we should never ask "why", never question God in our suffering, even if he withdraws his presence and leaves us to suffer alone. Instead, we should accept his inscrutable providence, because he is God and we are men who cannot possibly understand the mystery of his ways. The literature of piety is filled with prayers and hymns and sermons and meditations to that effect. Never question God, never contend with him, simply accept what he sends—that is the way of faith.

Is it really the way of faith? Surely faith is believing that God loves us and that everything he does is for our good. If he leaves us alone to suffer, if he seems to forsake us in the darkness, if he manifests himself as an absence rather than a presence, there must be a reason and it must be a loving reason. The way of faith is to reach out for that reason, reach out for God, cling to him, contend with him, ask him "why" and keep on asking until the darkness has been dispersed and the meaning has been made plain.

There was a hospital chaplain in Texas who advised a heartbroken couple to contend with God. Their teen-age daughter, who was everything that parents want a teen-age girl to be, became seriously ill and had to be taken to the hospital. Her illness was not definitely diagnosed, though it did not seem critical. When the parents arrived at the hospital one morning, a nurse met them in the corridor with the dreadful news that their daughter had died a few minutes earlier. It was like hitting them with a sledgehammer. The nurse didn't know what to say in that terrible moment so she asked if they would like to wait in the chapel. They sat together in the back pew, struggling with their thoughts. The chaplain entered but wisely refrained from offering them the usual and expected words of comfort. Instead, he went directly to the altar and knelt to pray for a few moments. As he was leaving he chapel he paused by their side long enough to say to them, "Go ahead and be mad at God. He's big enough to take it."[2] Contend with God, ask him "why?". That is the way of faith.

When we set the cry of dereliction in the context of the 22nd Psalm we hear it as *a cry of triumph*. At verse 22 the mood changes abruptly from prayer to praise and from grief to glory. The day has broken, the shadows have fled away, and in the new dawn of God's presence the man who uttered a cry of despair now sings a hymn of glad thanksgiving. *"I will declare thy name unto my brethren: in the midst of the congregation will I praise thee."* The rest of the Psalm may once have been a separate piece, but it was surely a part of the Psalm as Jesus knew it and began to recite it from the Cross. If it did fill his mind during those terrible dark hours, then he must have seen beyond the darkness to the light and seen the Psalmist's victory as a promise of his own. Let the Psalmist himself describe that victory.
"Ye that fear the Lord, praise him; all ye the seed of Jacob, glorify him; and fear him, all ye the seed of Israel." Here is a vision of all God's people engaged in a great act of praise. On the earthly scene it is a prelude to the hymns of the faithful coming from great city cathedrals and small country conventicles, from the African jungles and the frozen wastes of the north. On the heavenly scene it points to the vision of the author of the Book of Revelation: "And I beheld, and I heard the voice of many angels round about the throne . . . and the number of them was ten thousand times ten thousand, and thousands of thousands; Saying with a loud voice, Worthy is the Lamb that was slain to receive power, and riches, and wisdom, and strength, and honour, and glory, and blessing." (5:11–12 AV)
"The meek shall eat and be satisfied: they shall praise the Lord that seek him: your heart shall live forever." Here is a thank-offering meal that surely points to the Holy Communion which has been the central act of the church's worship for two thousand years.

Someone has said, "In that long space of time how many crowns and thrones have gone whistling down the wind! Yet this feast abides – a deep, cool well for the thirst of the generations." To this life-giving meal we come, in the words of Thomas à Kempis, "as those sick to the healer, hungry and thirsty to the fountain of life, needy to the king of heaven, servants unto their lord, creatures to their creator, desolate souls to a merciful comforter". We celebrate the sacrifice and the victory of one who cried from his Cross, "My God, my God, why hast thou forsaken me?"

"*All the ends of the world shall remember and turn unto the Lord: and all the kindreds of the nations shall worship before thee.*" The Psalmist sees the conversion of the whole earth, a vision which has found fulfilment in the World Church, called by William Temple "the great new fact of our time". Anyone who has been present at an Assembly of the World Council of Churches has seen the fulfilment of the hope expressed in the 22nd Psalm. It may not mean that the last person in the farthest corner of the world will turn to the God of the Bible and worship him. It does mean, however, that Christ is praised today by people of every language, race and colour and that all the kindreds of the nations have heard the message of the Cross.

"*They shall come, and shall declare his righteousness unto a people that shall be born, that he hath done this.*" The great accomplishment of the church has always been to preserve the faith and hand it on enriched to "a people that shall be born". The miracle is not the flexibility of the Gospel but its constancy, the fact that faith in the mighty acts of God is a source of blessing today as it was two thousand years ago. When all the wealth, all the wisdom, all the techniques and all the social panaceas have been exhausted, the greatest gift that one generation can bequeath to another is still the belief in "God the Father Almighty, Maker of heaven and earth, and in Jesus Christ his only Son our Lord . . ."

If Jesus saw all of that from his Cross when he began to recite the 22nd Psalm, then he was looking beyond his death to his Resurrection, because those are the fruits of the Resurrection, and his intensely human cry was a cry not only of faith but of victory. It can be our victory, as it was for old Dilsy, the Negro "mammy" in William Faulkner's novel, *The Sound and the Fury*. She served the decadent Compson family, all of whom broke

down under suffering while she alone stood up to the sound and
fury of life with tenderness and courage. There could be no
more apt description of the Dilsys of the world than that which
Faulkner gives them, "They endured". Dilsy found the secret
of her endurance in the powerful Easter sermon of a Negro
preacher who proclaimed a promise that gave her hope and
sustained the large spirit in her fatigued and debilitated body:
"I sees de resurrection en de light; sees de meek Jesus sayin,
Dey kilt me dat ye shall live again; I died dat dem what sees en
believes shall never die. Bredderen, O bredderen! I sees de
doom crack en hears de golden horns shouting down de glory,
en de arisen dead what got de blood en de ricklickshun of de
Lamb".[3] Beyond the darkness of Good Friday shines the brilliant light of Easter Day.

NOTES TO PSALM 22

1. London, Jonathan Cape, 1948; New York, Scribner, 1948.
2. Told by Robert E. Gooderich, Jr., in *Old Fires on New Altars*, ed. Wilson O. Weldon,
    (The Institute for Homiletical Studies, Western North Carolina Annual Confer-
    ence, The United Methodist Church, 1972) p. 114.
3. Random House Inc., New York, 1946; Chatto and Windus, London, pp. 312–313.

Psalm 24

He Feels Unworthy

This birthday card belongs to the category of "What will they think of next?" On the front is a picture of an eternally young angel with wings on her back, a halo on her head, a flower in her hand and a pleased smile on her face, standing on a cloud. The caption reads, "Only a person with a clean mind and a pure heart can open this birthday card." Nobody can open it, however, because the two sides are glued together. When you turn it around you see the same angel with a sheepish grin on her face. The caption reads, "Oh well, have a Happy Birthday anyway."

That could be a joke or it could be a lesson in Biblical theology. The mind goes immediately to a scene in the last book of the Bible where a strong angel in heaven proclaims with a loud voice, "Who is worthy to open the scroll and break its seals?" (Rev 5:2 RSV). Even more familiar are the question and answer in the 24th Psalm which the birthday card almost quotes accurately: *"Who shall ascend into the hill of the Lord? or who shall stand in his holy place? He that hath clean hands, and a pure heart; who hath not lifted up his soul unto vanity, nor sworn deceitfully."*

Who is worthy to enter the presence of God? That is the question raised by the writer of the 24th Psalm. Whether it puzzles us and whether or not it becomes a problem depends on how magnificently we think of God. If we think of him as a little God, a celestial choreboy loafing around his universe and pitifully pleading to be made use of, we can easily and casually saunter into his presence. But what if we think of him as a great

God? What if he is the King, the Creator and Supreme Owner of the Universe? The Psalm begins with that magnificent assertion: "*The earth is the Lord's, and the fullness thereof; the world, and they that dwell therein. For he hath founded it upon the seas, and established it upon the floods.*"

That is a daring and revolutionary assertion which challenges the human heart at a very sensitive point—the pride of ownership. That particular problem has triggered off nearly every major and minor war in history and even today brings races and nations to the brink of conflict. Who has legal right to the West Bank of the River Jordan? Who owns the oil beneath the floor of the ocean? Who can lay claim to the surface of the moon? The Psalmist answers those questions. He declares that God owns them all. God is the supreme owner of the universe, of the stars in their courses, the planet on which we dwell, its natural resources, history and peoples. All belong to him. They are his by right of creation and providence. That is a magnificent view of God, and when we think of him in those terms we realise that it is no easy and common thing to come into his presence. This is the God whom we dare to approach in our private prayer and public worship. Who is worthy to approach him?

The answer comes back, "He that hath clean hands, and a pure heart; who hath not lifted up his soul unto vanity, nor sworn deceitfully." That disqualifies some of us right away. A few saintly folk may squeeze by, but most people would be embarrassed if they were subjected to that rigid four-way test every time they tried to cross the threshold of a church. There was a lusty parish priest who one Christmas Eve stood at the church door and administered a human breathalyser test to all his parishioners who came to receive the Holy Communion. Those who exuded excessive alcohol fumes were turned away. How much better would any of us fare if we were tested by the stern standards of the 24th Psalm? Clean hands? Whose hands are clean of the corporate guilt of all mankind? Pure heart? Who can pretend that all his motives are transparently sincere? Not lifted up his soul unto vanity? Whose heart does not sometimes long after that which is empty and false? Nor sworn deceitfully? It is a rare person who everywhere and in all circumstances tells the unvarnished truth. To be sure, the favoured few who pass the test will "*receive the blessing from the Lord, and righteousness from the God of their salvation*", but the majority will be left standing outside.

Presumably that is where the Psalmist stood. He belonged to those of whom he said, "*This is the generation of them that seek him, that seek thy face, O Jacob.*" Yet he did not see the face of the God whom he sought because he felt unworthy to approach him. That was his reaction to his own magnificent view of God. He failed the test: and most of us, if we are honest, will identify with him. How can we approach fire when we are not fireproof? The only prayer we can offer is that of the mystic who said, "O God, Holy above all thought, Holy past all vision, Holy beyond all bearing; how can we ask to look upon Thy face, how could we stand in Thy presence, how shall we abide the very thought of Thee?" We too should be left standing outside, if the 24th Psalm ended there.

The original Psalm did end there. By a stroke of spiritual genius, however, the Jewish temple liturgy combined it with another Psalm, and the complete product appears in the Old Testament Psalter. Scholars have different opinions about who composed it and when, but all agree that it was used at one of the great temple feasts, probably the festival of New Year when God's people celebrated his enthronement as King of the world. The second part seems to be an antiphonal song that was sung by two choirs, one of which approaches the temple gates in solemn procession carrying the sacred ark or some other symbol of the presence of God and chanting, "*Lift up your heads, O ye gates; and be ye lift up, ye everlasting doors; and the King of glory shall come in.*" The other choir from within the temple sings, "*Who is this King of glory?*" The first choir responds, "*The Lord strong and mighty, the Lord mighty in battle . . . The Lord of hosts, he is the King of glory.*"

The Psalm not only answers the question, "Who shall ascend into the hill of the Lord? or who shall stand in his holy place?" but introduces the person who is himself the answer. If it is "he that hath clean hands, and a pure heart; who hath not lifted up his soul unto vanity, nor sworn deceitfully", then it must be a perfect person who shares the perfection of God. As far as we know, only one person in history fulfils those sublime conditions—Jesus, the God-Man, the Christ, the King of glory. He alone is worthy to approach the presence of God.

We can understand why the church has borrowed this old temple liturgy and used it in some of the great Christian festivals. It could have been written for Palm Sunday. On that day the church joins the procession going down the Mount of Olives, across the Kedron valley and up the other side toward the golden gate of the city. Jesus rides ahead of his disciples on a borrowed donkey. The children cluster around him and shout their hosannas. Some eager townsfolk lay their garments across his path, others wave branches, and the passing pilgrims cry, "Blessed is he who comes in the name of the Lord! Hosanna in the highest!" (Matt 21:9 RSV). On Palm Sunday the church sings the Psalm of approach: "Lift up your heads, O ye gates; and be ye lift up, ye everlasting doors; and the King of glory shall come in." To the question, "Who is this King of glory?" the church in its faith replies, "The Lord Jesus, strong and mighty, the Lord mighty in battle. He alone has clean hands and a pure heart. He alone is worthy to ascend into the hill of the Lord and stand in his holy place."

Or the Psalm could have been written for Ascension Day. Christ has been raised from the dead, he has created his church, he has finished the work that God gave him to do. From his lonely Cross came the cry that signalled both the end and the fulfilment of his earthly life, "It is accomplished!" (John 19:30 NEB). Having lived for a time in the devil's wild country, having fought and defeated all the powers of evil on the devil's own ground, Christ has proved himself to be the Lord strong and mighty, the Lord mighty in battle. Now he returns to the heavenly glory from which he came. As he approaches the gates of heaven, a choir of angels sings, "Lift up your heads, O ye gates; and be ye lift up, ye everlasting doors; and the King of glory shall come in." To the question, "Who is this King of glory?" the choir replies, "The Lord of hosts, he who has clean hands and a pure heart. He alone of all people who ever walked the earth has not lifted up his soul unto vanity nor sworn deceitfully. He alone is worthy to approach God."

That does indeed answer the Psalmist's question, "Who shall ascend into the hill of the Lord?" but it does not answer the question *for us*. It does not bring the 24th Psalm any closer to real life or dispel our sense of unworthiness to approach God. There is frustration as well as fascination in watching a joyous, triumphal procession, especially if we want to be a part of it but know ourselves disqualified. A person may feel that frustration on a Royal occasion when he watches the élite few filing into Westminster Abbey. He would like to enter the Abbey and be in the presence of Her Majesty the Queen but he is not qualified. He can only join the applause of the crowds that line the route outside. The pilgrim to Rome feels the same frustration when he watches the Pope, followed by Cardinals and Bishops, processing into St. Peter's. He too would like to enter the historic church but he doesn't have a ticket, so he can only join the shouting multitudes that pack St. Peter's Square. Palm Sunday and Ascension Day are joyous, triumphal occasions in the church's life but they celebrate the joy and triumph of Christ. How do they avail for us? How do we qualify to join the triumphal procession of those who are worthy to approach the presence of God?

Perhaps we shall answer that question if we consider the use of the 24th Psalm in another great Christian festival, the festival of Christmas. "Lift up your heads, O ye gates; and be ye lift up, ye everlasting doors; and the King of glory shall come in." At Christmas the King of glory divested himself of heavenly glory and came into our world. As he approached the stronghold of human hearts and society, a choir of angels sang, "Lift up your heads, O ye gates—the gates of human pride, human suffering, entrenched evil and tyrannical death—and the King of glory shall come in." That is a reversal of the movement of the Psalm. It does not answer the question, Who is worthy to approach the presence of God? It eliminates the question altogether.

Christmas celebrates the truth that we don't have to be worthy to approach God, because he approaches us and comes where we are. It celebrates the "condescension" of God, which is not a patronising word; actually it derives from the verb "to condescend" which means "to waive one's superiority and step down". In that sense condescension is a sign of greatness. When Abraham Lincoln was President of the United States he was always sacrificing his superiority and stepping down to meet people on their own ground. He sometimes called on his colleagues at their homes instead of summoning them to the White House. On one occasion the insolent General McClellan sent word by a servant that he was too tired to see the President. Lincoln's response was that he would "hold General McClellan's stirrup for him if only he will win us victories".

Such was God's gracious condenscension, multiplied to infinity. We can believe that God looked upon his world and saw an ever-widening gulf between himself and his earthly children. He saw the religions of the world shrouding him in mystery and making him less and less accessible to ordinary people. The religion of the Jews secluded him behind a curtain in an empty space which only one man, the High Priest, could enter one day a year. God said, "Soon none of my children will be considered or consider himself good enough to approach me. I must go to them. The gulf must be bridged from my side." So on Christmas Eve the cry sounded forth from heaven, "Lift up your heads, all you people who feel unworthy to approach God. This day God is about to approach you."

Christmas celebrates the truth that, when God did approach the world he came not in majesty and power but in lowliness and humility. Even children don't always grasp that truth, though they may ask the right questions. A school teacher in England tells of supervising the construction of a Christmas manger scene in the corner of the classroom. She and the pupils set up a model barn and covered the floor with real straw and arranged clay figures of Mary and Joseph and the Shepherds and the Wise Men, all facing a little crib that contained a tiny doll representing the Baby Jesus. One pupil kept returning to it and stood there completely engrossed, wearing a puzzled expression on his face. At length the teacher noticed him and asked, "Is anything bothering you? Do you have a question to ask? What would you like to know?" His eyes still glued to the manger scene, the boy said slowly, "What I'd like to know is—where does God fit in?"

That was a reverent, mature and profoundly religious question to ask at Christmas. Where does God fit in? That lowly manger scene contradicts everything we have always believed about God and everything we imagine about his entrance into the world. Suppose you had been present on Christmas Eve and the angels had announced to you, as they did to the

shepherds, that on that very night "the King of glory shall come
in", how would you expect him to come? Could you describe in
words the awesomeness, the majesty and the regal splendour of
your expectations? You would surely assume that God, when
he comes, must look like God, brighter than the sun, riding in a
chariot more glistening than one set with ten thousand
diamonds, flanked and followed by the heavenly host of chanting angels, led by the archangels with their fiery swords.

We are back to the grandeur of Westminster Abbey and St.
Peter's. How could we ever get close to that awesome and
frightening Deity? Who would dare to approach him on Mount
Olympus or in Caesar's palace or at the temple in Jerusalem,
for surely in one of those exalted places he would take up
residence? Yet we dare to approach a Bethlehem stable where
straw litters the floor and animals sleep in their stalls and
peasants gather to adore a new-born baby. Even the lowliest
child can approach the God who comes to meet us there. If the
child asks, "Where does God fit in?" we shall answer, "This *is*
God, this little Baby nestled in his mother's arms. It is a new
kind of almightiness. It is God's way of coming into the world
and of being with us, so that we might be with him and love and
trust him."

Christmas celebrates the truth that we don't have to open the
birthday card, because Christ has opened it. Christmas is the
story of a birthday—not the anniversary of a birth but the
birthday itself. We go to the maternity ward to visit the mother
and the baby. God is present there, as he is always present at
the birth of a child, yet present in a very special way. His
presence fills the place like smoke, just as it once filled the
temple, so that the young Isaiah cried out, "Woe is me! for I am
undone; because I am a man of unclean lips, and I dwell in the
midst of a people of unclean lips: for mine eyes have seen the
King, the Lord of hosts." (Isa 6:5 AV) In the temple Isaiah was
asking, in effect, "Who is worthy to be in the presence of God?"
In the stable at Bethlehem we don't have to ask that question.
We can have a happy birthday anyway.

That's because the story did not end in Bethlehem but
continued to Nazareth and Galilee and Jerusalem and a skull-
shaped hill outside a city wall. There the Lord of glory proved
himself to be the Lord strong and mighty, the Lord mighty in

battle. There he won the victory over sin and death that qualified him to enter heaven and to "open the scroll and break its
seals". He won that victory for us, on our behalf, in our place.
We don't have to stand by as disqualified spectators and simply
watch the triumphal procession that approaches the presence
of God. Our Lord takes us with him in the procession. We don't
have to be worthy to open the birthday card, because he is
worthy. The saints in heaven sing of his worthiness: "Worthy
art thou to take the scroll and to open its seals, for thou wast
slain and by thy blood didst ransom men for God." (Rev 5:9
RSV) We can have a happy birthday anyway.

Psalm 32

He Feels Happy

"*Blessed is he whose transgression is forgiven . . .*" The keyword is
"blessed". It has a larger, deeper, richer, more spiritual meaning than "happy" (NEB), yet blessedness contains happiness
as a red hot iron contains fire. That gives the Psalm a very
human appeal and brings it right into our experience. Most
people want to be happy. They dream of happiness, they plan
for it and will often pay any price to achieve it. In the search for
happiness one man makes a lot of money, and another gives all
his money away. In the same search one woman has half a
dozen babies, and another goes into a convent. Ask the average
person what he wants most out of life, and the chances are that
he will reply without hesitation, "I want to be happy."

The 32nd Psalm contains the spiritual case-history of a man
who discovered a way to happiness. To him that was a vitally
important discovery, because he had not been happy; in fact, he
had been quite miserable. He tells about three stages in his
experience, the first a stage of *abject misery*. It was the misery of a
painful and serious illness. He does not specify its exact nature
but he does describe the symptoms. He says, "*. . . my bones
waxed old through my roaring all the day long . . . my moisture is turned
into the drought of summer.*" The New English Bible puts it, "my
body is wasted away". It is a terrible thing for any person to see
his own body wasting away and to realise that some day there
will be nothing left and he will die.

There could be no doubt in anybody's mind about the cause
of his illness. According to the settled opinion of the times he
was guilty of some sin, else he would not have fallen ill. The

Jews connected all sickness with sin. They argued inexorably that if a man suffered he must be a sinner. Openly or secretly, knowingly or ignorantly he must have broken God's laws, and God was punishing him for it. Job's so-called "comforters" pressed that point almost brutally, "Who ever perished, being innocent?" (Job 4:7 AV). Job himself had a more enlightened view. He insisted that his suffering might have nothing to do with sin, a view that Jesus confirmed when he answered the question of his disciples concerning the man born blind, "It was not that this man sinned, or his parents . . ." (John 9:3 RSV). Yet even Jesus cured a paralysed man by saying, "My son, your sins are forgiven." (Mark 2:5 RSV) He may not have believed that crude theology but he knew that the man himself believed it and that no power in the world could make him stand up and walk until someone persuaded him that God had forgiven his sins.

Even today there is nothing fanciful about the connection between suffering and sin. It may not be as direct and automatic as people assumed in Old Testament times but it is still present in varying degrees. The sense of guilt lays a burden on the soul, and the soul passes part of the burden to the body, and the patient becomes physically ill. A medical doctor, S. I. McMillen, wrote a little book called *None of These Diseases*[1] based on the promise that God made to the Israelites when he brought them out of slavery in Egypt. If they would obey his commandments and statutes, he would put "none of these diseases" upon them. (Exodus 15:26 AV) McMillen examines a number of common diseases—high blood pressure, toxic goitre, migraine headaches, arthritis, apoplexy, heart trouble, peptic ulcers, and many others—which may be caused by our failure to obey God's laws. Modern medical science acknowledges a very definite connection between suffering and sin.

The Psalmist, conditioned by orthodox theology, knew that there was such a connection but in his own case he refused to admit it. Like the suffering Job he persuaded himself that no sins could be charged against him. He admitted that God was the author of his suffering—"*For day and night thy hand was heavy upon me . . .*"—but he refused to believe that he deserved it. God was punishing him unjustly. His friends may have begged him to search his conscience and pour out a prayer of confession, but he *"kept silence"*. That was a very human thing to do. Not many people, suffering from emotional or physical illness, are prepared to admit that they have brought it upon themselves by their disobedience of God's laws. More likely they make the rounds of the medical profession, hoping that a new drug or a series of treatments or even an operation will give them back their health. They would be surprised if some kindly doctor said what Shakespeare's doctor said concerning Lady Macbeth, "More needs she the divine than the physician."

That's what Dr. Paul Tournier, the Swiss psychiatrist, told a patient whom he visited in hospital. "My dear friend," he said, "I have come to tell you frankly what is the matter with you." With unremitting frankness he then pinpointed the patient's problem as a psychotic sense of guilt over a tragedy for which he felt responsible. "You have come to a crossroads," said Dr. Tournier. "I have no doubt that God has brought you to this present moment so that you can make your choice. There are two roads in front of you. One goes from clinic to clinic; it is full of suffering, but it is relatively easy to take. It is the road along which you expect healing to come from others, from doctors clever enough to discover some new remedy which will cure you." Dr. Tournier went on, "The other road is very much harder. It is the road to Jesus Christ, who has warned us that it is a narrow and difficult one. If you take it, you must accept what comes to you, carry your cross, go back to work, and face up to life even though it hurts. It is a road which demands a change of heart. But you do not travel it alone; and even if it demands the greatest sacrifices, you will find joy in it, because as you go you will find that Christ is at your side, and your sins are forgiven."[2]

Perhaps someone gave similar advice to the Psalmist in his illness. He may even have said it to himself but he did nothing about it. He kept silence. Meanwhile his pain became more intense, his body more emaciated, and his chances of survival more faint. Abject misery was the first stage in his spiritual history.

The second stage can be described as *moral honesty before God*. Came the day when the poor fellow could suffer no longer. He had to break his silence or die. *"I acknowledged my sin unto thee, and mine iniquity have I not hid.*" He didn't simply break down like a torture victim and confess a guilt which he did not feel. He actually searched his conscience and found the particular sin which he had committed and confessed it to God. "*I said, I will confess my transgressions unto the Lord; and thou forgavest the iniquity of my sin.*" That was probably the most painful thing he ever did but also the most liberating because it marked the turning point in his experience. From that moment his condition began to improve. Whether the sin that he confessed had actually caused his illness or not, the very act of moral honesty before God became a healing force in his body and soul.

The New Testament has a shorthand word for moral honesty before God, the word "repentance". It was the main theme of John the Baptist who came "preaching a baptism of repentance for the forgiveness of sins". (Luke 3:3 RSV) Jesus preached a Gospel of repentance: "The time is fulfilled, and the kingdom of God is at hand; repent, and believe in the gospel." (Mark 1:15 RSV) There are two movements in the act of repentance, a turning *from* sin and a turning *to* God. The repentant sinner returns to God as the prodigal son returned to his father and makes the same confession, "I have sinned against heaven, and in thy sight, and am no more worthy to be called thy son." (Luke 15:21 AV) That was the turning point in *his* experience. It may have been painful and humiliating but it was also healing and liberating because it took him out of his misery and opened for him a new way to happiness.

Augustine in the fourth century made that same thrilling discovery. It is reported that he had the 32nd Psalm inscribed above his bed so that he could read it first thing every morning. He had made the Psalmist's experience his own. His great book, *The Confessions*, one of the devotional classics of the world, records the moral honesty of a human conscience before God. He also felt wretched in body and soul but refused to believe that it was caused by his own intellectual pride and by a dissolute lifestyle that separated him from God. The crisis came as he sat weeping under a fig tree and heard a voice from a neighbouring house which said, "Take read". In his hand was a copy of Paul's Epistles. He says, "I seized it, opened it, and read in silence the passage upon which my eyes first fell: 'not in rioting and drunkenness, not in chambering and wantonness, not in strife and envying, but put ye on the Lord Jesus Christ and make no provision for the flesh to fulfil the lusts thereof'." Augustine adds, "I cared not to read further, nor was there need. For all at once, as I came to the end of the sentence, my heart was filled with a sunshine of confidence, before which all my dark doubts fled away." That was the turning point in his experience. Moral honesty before God became for him, as it did for the Psalmist, a way to happiness.

That would delight the Psalmist's heart. Having found a way to happiness, he wants to share it, especially with the young and inexperienced. He says specifically, *"I will instruct thee and teach thee in the way which thou shalt go . . ."* He calls upon all who are godly to cultivate and practise the habit of prayer and return to God, not as animals who have to be bridled but as human beings who can come by choice. His words may be paraphrased: "If you are ill or suffering any kind of physical or emotional misery, consider the possibility that you brought it upon yourself by your disobedience of God's laws. Go into the secret place of your heart. Unlock the hidden door. Take out the unresolved guilt, the unforgiven sin. Be morally honest about it before God, confess it to him, repent. It won't be easy, but you will recover your health of body and mind and you will set your feet on the way to happiness."

Happiness is the third stage in the Psalmist's spiritual history. After he had been morally honest with God, his whole mood changed as the whole earth changes when the sunlight comes out after a storm. Yet it was not he himself but God who made him happy. His happiness was an emotional response to God's forgiveness, a total and complete forgiveness which he describes in four memorable phrases.

"Blessed is he whose transgression is forgiven . . ." Transgression implies wilful disobedience against some kind of legal or moral authority. Forgiveness is a personal act whereby the transgressor, because of his penitence, is freely restored to the relationship in which he stood before he defied that authority. It happens in family life all the time and must happen if family life is to be happy. A newspaper in Britain showed a photograph of a husband and wife, arm in arm, sublimely happy and smiling at each other with an expression of mutual trust. It was entitled

"Reconciliation" and it told a heart-warming story. This woman, in a strange lapse of character, had been unfaithful to her husband and had actually deserted him and the children and gone to live with her lover. Like the prodigal son she "came to herself", saw the wretchedness of her condition and returned to her husband who freely restored her to his home and his heart. That is how God receives the penitent sinner. That is what the Bible means by forgiveness. It is a way to happiness.

"Blessed is he . . . whose sin is covered." There is a moving example of that in Charles Dickens' novel, *David Copperfield*, where Little Emily runs away from home, leaving a note confessing that she is pregnant. Her uncle, Mr. Peggoty, resolves to find her. He tells the woman whose son seduced Emily, "I'm a-going to seek her, fur and wide . . . If I should bring her back again, my meaning is, that she and me shall live and die where no one can't reproach her." He does exactly that. He finds Emily in a life of shame, takes her out of it and emigrates with her to Australia to a new life where no one can reproach her. He covers her sin. God's forgiveness is like that. Dwight L. Moody used to say that God has put our sins not only where we can't see them, he has put them where he can't see them. He covers them. We only insult the grace of God and increase our own misery when we refuse to do the same thing. When sins are catastrophic in their effects, it takes a mighty exercise of faith to believe that God covers them, but such faith is a way to happiness.

"Blessed is the man unto whom the Lord imputeth not iniquity . . ." That means that the Lord lays no guilt to his account. Nothing stands against him even in the unforgiving region of law. There is no eternal dossier that contains an indelible record of all his misdeeds and failures. Some people fear that there is. They cannot suppress the feeling that their sins, although forgiven and covered, are somehow chalked up against them like traffic offences on the back of a driver's licence. If they pile up too many offences, they might even lose the licence. Perhaps they will never know the truth until they stand before the great King on his throne and he shows them the page on which the offence was written and they see that it is a clean page. The record may have been there once but it has been erased and the page wiped clean. Then they will realise how much happier their lives

would have been if they had accepted God's complete forgiveness—which means that in the sight of God it is as though they never committed the sin at all.

"*Blessed is the man . . . in whose spirit there is no guile.*" That means no deceit, no possibility of the sin's recurrence. A surgeon can give the greatest happiness to a person who has undergone a cancer operation by telling him that all traces of the malignancy have been removed. The disease has been cured, and the symptoms will not recur. That's what made the Psalmist happy. Like a radical and excruciatingly painful operation God's forgiveness had cured him not only of sin but of sinfulness, that inner falsehood, that deceit, that guile which, exposed to temptation, could start the whole vicious circle all over again. The Apostle Paul shared the Psalmist's happiness. He saw sin not only as a series of symptoms but as a deep-seated moral malignancy that had to be cut away. He cried out, "Wretched man that I am! Who will deliver me from this body of death?" His answer was a shout of joy, "Thanks be to God through Jesus Christ our Lord!" (Rom 7:24, 25 RSV).

Inevitably we come into the presence of Jesus Christ our Lord, inevitably to the foot of the Cross. The 32nd Psalm points to the Cross. It holds out the promise of God's forgiveness which the Cross makes actual and inserts into human experience. Whoever comes to the Cross of Jesus Christ in absolute moral honesty will receive from God a total and complete forgiveness that restores his health of body and soul and opens for him a new way to happiness. To all who stand before the Cross the Psalmist sings, "*Be glad in the Lord, and rejoice, ye righteous: and shout for joy, all ye that are upright in heart.*"

NOTES TO PSALM 32

1. Spire Books, Fleming H. Revell Company, Westwood, New Jersey.
2. Paul Tournier, *The Healing of Persons* (New York: Harper & Row, 1965) p. 217.

Psalm 39

He Feels Desperate

When a person says that he is not getting any younger, though he says it with a smile on his face, the chances are that he is beginning to feel just a little desperate. He has probably reached and passed the age where he expected certain things to happen and he knows that if they don't happen soon they won't happen at all, because he will be too old for them. Disappointed in love, a woman may say, "The right man will have to come along soon, because I am not getting any younger." Frustrated in his work, a man may say, "If something doesn't develop in this job, I'll have to look for another one because I am not getting any younger." Held down by ill-health, overwork, financial debt, an unhappy marriage or the care of aged relatives, a person may exclaim, "If I don't get a chance to enjoy life soon, it will be too late, because I am not getting any younger." Such people are not being unreasonable. They don't expect to get any younger, they don't resent the passing of time. What they do resent is that their time is running out, life is passing them by, and they feel just a little desperate.

The author of the 39th Psalm felt desperate for the very same reason. Although his poem has been called "the noblest elegy of the Psalter", it reads like the product of a dejected mind and a heart torn by deep distress. His passionate complaint suggests that he may have suffered some severe blow, perhaps a physical illness or a crushing disappointment or simply an unbroken season of fruitless labour and hope deferred that breaks the morale of any man. Up to now he had kept quiet about it, presumably for two reasons. First, he knew that the complaint of a godly man does not make other people sorry for him but only heaps fuel on the fires of unbelievers. Second, he believed, as all devout Jews believed, that God sent all suffering as a punishment for sin. So there was no point complaining. Better that a person should do something about it, examine himself, make atonement, amend his ways, suffer in silence and wait for the situation to improve.

But the Psalmist's situation had not improved and it showed no signs of improving. Meanwhile, he was not getting any younger. He saw the best years of his life receding into the past, heard the knocking of opportunities that would never knock again, felt the ebbing away of strength that does not return. If happier days were coming they had better come soon. After all, life does not go on forever, and the good things of life are not much use to a person after he is dead or even too old to enjoy them. At length the Psalmist could contain himself no longer. All the bitterness which he had stoked in the silence burst forth into the flames of an angry prayer:

> Lord, let me know my end,
>   and what is the measure of my days;
>   let me know how fleeting my life is!
> Behold, thou hast made my days a few handbreadths,
>   and my lifetime is as nothing in thy sight.
>
> Hear my prayer, O Lord,
>   and give ear to my cry;
>   hold not thy peace at my tears!
> For I am thy passing guest,
>   a sojourner, like all my fathers.
> Look away from me, that I may
>   know gladness,
>   before I depart and be no more!
>   (RSV)

We detect a mood of panic in the 39th Psalm. We sense beneath it terseness and restraint a seething emotion that threatens to get out of hand and drive the man berserk. No question either about the source of his panic. It was the panic of the closed door. Though he does not use this exact imagery, the Psalmist evidently saw the whole of life as a period of imprisonment in a long rectangular room with a closed door at each end, the door behind him labelled "birth", and the door ahead of him labelled "death". Within that space he must live his allotted time and within those four walls he must work out his salvation. Whatever meanings and satisfactions life affords must be found within the confines of that long rectangular room.

The Hebrew poet did not take his situation lying down. Sometimes in the stillness he speculated and even hoped that beyond the door marked "death" there might be other rooms, other opportunities to resolve the puzzles and injustices of this life. Furtively perhaps he had tried the handle, given it a shake, leaned his weight against it in the effort to get a glimpse beyond, but no use. It was strongly bolted on the outside. Only once would that door open, and so far as the Psalmist knew, he would cross its threshold into the nothingness from which he had first come. In the morning hours, with most of life ahead of him, it had not mattered too much; but now with the hands of the clock well past midday and so few of his hopes realised, he felt himself becoming desperate. Hence his passionate plea to God, "Look away from me, that I may know gladness, before I depart and be no more."

We must not allow the over-all mood to obscure some of the positive lessons of the 39th Psalm. Because this ancient poem issued from a sense of constriction between birth and death it deserves to be called "the noblest elegy of the Psalter". Arrestingly the poet recalls us to the fleeting nature of human life and the brevity of our time upon this earth. Dramatically he reminds us that we do not own the long rectangular room, nor can we remain in it indefinitely. The room belongs to God. We are his guests. He invited us to stay and he expects us to leave; and while we are here we should behave like well-mannered guests. The Old Testament poet refuses to make the closed door an excuse for careless and selfish living. He will live for significant ends regardless of the brevity of his existence. Even if death means annihilation, he will die knowing it better to have lived worthily than not to have lived at all. We may credit him with the nobility of Lord Bertrand Russell who said, "Happiness is none the less true happiness because it must

come to an end, nor do thought and love lose their value
because they are not everlasting."

Then why did the Psalmist feel desperate? What troubled
him and threw him into panic? Surely the suspicion that Russell's viewpoint, however noble, is ultimately not true; the
suspicion that happiness, thought and love do lose their value if
they are not everlasting. The Psalmist felt about life as one
drama critic felt about a television play. He said that there were
some meanings *in* it but no meaning *to* it. As a religious man he
believed that only God can give meaning to life, but, as far as he
could see, his relationship with God ended at the closed door. If
God had a purpose for him, that purpose must be fulfilled in
this world; if God dealt justly with a person, his justice must be
worked out in that person's lifetime; whatever blessings the
Father God visited upon his children must be visited here and
now. It all stopped at the closed door. Beyond that door the
purpose, the justice and the blessings of God did not reach, so
that in the end they all added up to nothing; and if the end of life
is nothing, then life itself, the preface to that end, is nothing.
That is what troubled the Psalmist and threw him into panic.

There is only one answer to the Psalmist's prayer, and that is
a hope of personal immortality. Somehow he must see life in a
larger perspective, over-arching the brief span of his earthly
existence. He must see the long rectangular room as only one
room in God's house and he must see the closed door as an
entrance to other rooms. He must come to realise that God's
Providence reaches beyond our earthly lifetime and is not
frustrated by our experience of death. He must know that God
has all eternity in which to fulfil his purpose and work out his
justice and visit his blessings on any person.

It seems strange that this "noblest elegy of the Psalter",
which reaches sublime heights of religious devotion, offers not a
glimmer of hope in life beyond the grave. Of course, the obvious
explanation is an historical one. The Hebrew poet lived too
soon, six centuries too soon. "Ah, my heavy-hearted friend,"
we say to him, "you need to learn that the God to whom you
poured out your complaint is the God and Father of our Lord
Jesus Christ. You need to learn that your God has once and for
all put an end to vague, shadowy speculations about im-

mortality and has brought life and immortality to life through the Gospel. You need to hear the comforting words of Jesus, 'In my Father's house are many rooms . . . I go to prepare a place for you.'[1] And you need to be told that Jesus did indeed pass through that closed door at the end of the room and came back again to tell us of the other rooms beyond." Thus we should reassure the writer of the 39th Psalm if with the aid of a time-machine we could travel back through the centuries, knowing what we know now.

Whether we should convince him depends upon whether we are convinced ourselves. Suppose the Old Testament poet, after listening to our New Testament arguments, replied, "I am a reasonably intelligent man. I should like to believe you, of course, because if what you say is true, it changes everything. You promise me that I need not realise the purpose of life in time, because God has all eternity in which to work. That's an exciting promise, but I wonder if you believe it yourself. Let me try to find out. Let me come with you into your twentieth century. Let me watch you as each day you grow older. Let me read your books, listen to your prayers and see how you react to the crises that threw me into panic."

Having said that, suppose the Psalmist picked up a newspaper or walked into a library or a theatre and began studying what we call our "culture", man's interpretation in art and letters of his own situation. To take an extreme case, suppose he read a book, published a few years ago, entitled *The Beat Generation and the Angry Young Men*, advertised as representing "many of the most brilliant and significant writers of our times". That book reflects the panic of the closed door. It begins with the cynical statement that in a world of ultimate weapons there is no point hoping in the future, because we have no future. And let's not be fooled by the fact that life seems to go on normally. As the writer says,

> The facade of this present seeming normalcy shows signs of weathering; each day the mortar crumbles a little more. Man, behind the masks with which he plays his daily roles, cannot be totally blind to the continuing collapse . . . He glimpses the portents of

chaos everywhere and correspondingly grows aware of
his own nakedness and impotence—his nothingness.
His fate—survival or extinction—bears less relation to
his personal moral bookkeeping than to the scarcely
audible assents and dissents of power figures almost too
fear-stricken to make decisions. He senses that time is
shrinking into itself, the past losing its relevance and
the future receding further and further from his control.
Only the present seems to hold the possibility of his
meaningful participation, for he can still possess the
moment.[2]

Suppose the Psalmist turned from our culture to the social
idealism of our day, would he find that related to any frame of
eternal meaning? Instead, would he not find our political and
social thinking dominated by his own illusion, namely, that we
must live to see all our own strivings come to fruition, or life is a
cosmic blunder, and whose blunder? Emil Brunner, who
coined the phrase, "the panic of the closed door", called it
"Utopianism"—a friendly illusion, though in reality a terrible
thing. Having lost the hope of heaven, men try to create a
heaven on earth and sometimes they end up by creating a hell
instead. When man thinks that all his political and social goals
must be reached within his own lifetime, or even within history,
he panics and resorts to coercion and violence in order to
achieve them.[3] He is doing exactly that in the world today—in
the Far East, in the emerging nations of Africa, in Communist
Europe and even in the social and scientific planning of the
Christian West. The whole temper of modern society—its
violence, irrationality, disintegration and hatred—reflect the
panic of the closed door.

Suppose the Psalmist picked up a popular magazine which,
though not reflecting the highest in our culture, would initiate
him into a layman's view of modern medicine. He might read
the fabulous story of some wonder drug, as yet untried but
reputed to renew the body's protein molecules and arrest the
process of growing old. He could not help being impressed by
the marvels of medical science, though he might raise an eye-
brow at the fact that we do require drugs to live out a lesser span
of life than people in his day managed to live without the help of
drugs. In the light of our Christian hope of eternity he might

wonder at our excitement over scientific discoveries which promise to postpone eternity for ten or twenty years. They don't change our essential situation—we die eventually anyway; all that remains to be settled is the date—but the fact that we make such a fuss over them indicates that we do not accept our essential situation. Whatever orthodox beliefs lie on the top of our minds, deep down in our hearts we also are worried about the closed door and, as midnight approaches, we become just a little desperate.

Suppose the Psalmist slipped quietly into our home and spent an evening observing our family life and listening to the conversation. He might be amused at the nightly struggle to get the children to bed. "Please, Daddy, let me finish this puzzle." "No, I've told you five times to turn out the light." "But, Daddy, it will only take a few minutes." "I said No." "Oh Daddy, I do want to finish it before going to sleep." "Look, you've got all day tomorrow and the next day and the next day to work out that puzzle. Now go to bed!" "Well, that's that," you say, complimenting yourself, as you settle back comfortably and pick up the evening newspaper. Suddenly you go into the kitchen. "Look, dear," you exclaim to your wife in a shocked voice, handing her the paper, "Henry Jones just died. He had a heart attack at his summer cottage." For a long time you remain silent, unaware of a presence listening carefully to every word that you will say. What about your hope of heaven, your belief that a person can fall asleep peacefully at the end of life's day, knowing that he has all eternity in which to work out life's puzzle? Is it true? Do you really believe it? At last you express your real feelings, and what you say carries the overtones of panic. "Henry Jones was a good man. He didn't deserve to die so soon. He and his wife built that cottage so that they could retire there next year. All their lives they worked and saved. Now for the first time, with their children married and their debts paid off, they could have relaxed and enjoyed life for a while. It's a rotten shame!"

James Stewart caught that mood in a memorable sermon entitled "The Transformation of Tragedy" where he describes the eleven disciples in the Upper Room between Good Friday and Easter Day, their hearts frozen by despair, shame, fear and Christ-forsakenness. He says, "This broken, warring world is

living on the wrong side of Easter Day. That is the basic fact
and the source of all our troubles. We are back where the
disciples were. Like them, we are groping in the dark. We are
on the wrong side of Easter."[4] That may be true. After two
thousand years of the Christian Era it is still possible to be back
spiritually with the Old Testament Psalmist who cried out to
God, "Look away from me, that I may know gladness, before I
depart and be no more." It is also possible, through faith in
Christ, to sing the triumph song of the saints: "O death, where
is thy victory? O death, where is thy sting? . . . Thanks be to
God, who gives us the victory through our Lord Jesus Christ.
Therefore, my beloved brethren, be steadfast, immovable,
always abounding in the work of the Lord, knowing that in the
Lord your labour is not in vain." (1 Cor 15:55-58 RSV)

NOTES TO PSALM 39

1. John 14: 2 RSV.
2. *The Beat Generation and the Angry Young Men*, ed. Gene Feldman and Max Garten-
   berg, New York, Citadel Press, 1958.
3. Emil Brunner, *Faith, Hope and Love*, Philadelphia, The Westminster Press, 1956,
   pp. 53-54.
4. J. S. Stewart, *The Strong Name*, Edinburgh, T. & T. Clark, 1940, p. 35ff.

Psalm 40

He Feels Committed

The Old Testament Psalms were written by people whose experience of life was very much like our own. They were the kind of people with whom we can identify. They knew what it was to be afraid, to carry heavy burdens, to face danger, to be under stress and to feel their lives going in all directions at the same time. They did a very wise thing. They brought God into their experience and found that he did for them what no one else could do. God heartened them in their fears, supported them under their burdens, guarded them against danger, calmed them in their stress and unified their lives around his all-controlling purpose. The Psalms are a chronicle of God's activity in human experience. They tell us what we can expect of God.

They tell us also what God expects of us. They record not only the activity of God but man's reaction to that activity. They show how the Psalmists responded to God and how God wanted them to respond. The theme of this chapter might be called "The Response God Wants" and it raises an important question: How *does* God want us to respond when he enters our experience and does for us what no one else can do? We look for an answer in the 40th Psalm which bears so directly on that theme that it becomes a pattern for all the rest. On the one hand, the Psalmist tells exactly what God did for him. On the other hand, he tells exactly how he responded.

He describes his experience of God in picturesque detail:
"I waited patiently for the Lord; and he inclined unto me, and heard my cry. He brought me up also out of an horrible pit, out of the miry clay, and

*set my feet upon a rock, and established my goings. And he hath put a new
song in my mouth, even praise unto our God: many shall see it, and fear,
and shall trust in the Lord."*

Obviously the man had been in some kind of trouble. Scholars suggest that he was seriously ill and could feel himself sinking into the pit of Sheol, the world of the dead from which there is no return. He sent distress signals to God but didn't get an immediate reply. He says, "I waited patiently for the Lord"—though how patient can a person be when he is stuck in a bog and can feel the quicksand rising to his neck? At the last minute God came to his rescue, reached out a hand, pulled him out of the mire, set him on the solid ground of good health and restored him to his normal activities. From that moment he became a living advertisement for his religion. You can hear his friends whispering among themselves, "What's happened to him? Something, that's certain. He seems so different. Only yesterday he was moody and irritable. Nobody wanted him around. Now he's cheerful and happy. He sings hymns all the time. Nothing gets him down. Religion? Well, I never thought much about it, but you can't argue against religion when it does that for a person."

Religion does exactly that for a person. It did that for John Wesley. He had been bogged down in the horrible pit of despond, the miry clay of doubt. Though he was an ordained clergyman and erstwhile missionary, he felt himself paralysed by a sense of unreality. Passionately he prayed for a sense of what is vital in religion and patiently he waited for God to answer his prayer. God did answer him. One night in a little chapel in London, as he listened to the reading of Luther's Preface to Paul's Roman Epistle, the central meaning of the Gospel broke with overpowering conviction upon his soul, and he felt his heart strangely warmed. In that luminous hour he knew that God had brought him up out of the horrible pit, out of the miry clay, and had set his feet upon a rock and established his goings. God put a new song in his mouth, a song of praise that burst forth into some of our most joyous hymns.

> I'll praise my Maker while I've breath
> And when my voice is lost in death,
> Praise shall employ my nobler powers . . .

Many saw it and feared and trusted in the Lord. Out of Wesley's experience came a revival of religion that bequeathed to the world a new kind of Christianity and, according to historians, saved a whole nation from bloody revolution.

The experience shared by the Psalmist and John Wesley goes by the old-fashioned name of "salvation", a glorious word that used to mean as much in religion as the word "happiness" means in marriage. It seems to have disappeared from the vocabulary of mainline churches, the word as well as the idea; and that is a serious loss, because salvation is the very experience at the heart and centre of the Gospel. What happened to the Psalmist can be seen as a figure of the Gospel. Before Christ came, the whole human race was like a person who has fallen into a dark well and broken his legs in the fall. He cannot climb out to safety on a ladder of his own resolutions, because the ladder must be fastened at the top. Someone from above must come down to him in his darkness and help him upwards to the light. The good news of the Gospel is that Someone did come down. Jesus Christ was the hand of God that reached into our desperate situation and lifted us out of the horrible pit, out of the miry clay, and set our feet upon a rock and established our goings and put a new song in our mouth, even praise unto our God. Many myriads of millions have seen it and feared and have trusted in the Lord.

Having told what God did for him, the Psalmist now tells how he responded. First, he praised God, he sang a brief hymn declaring who it was that saved him. He says that in his distress he might have turned to foreign gods or demons and their human agents, but he made the Lord his trust and did not turn to the proud. After God saved him he went to church and merged his private praise with the public worship of the congregation who extolled the works of God and his care for the nation Israel. "*Many, O Lord my God, are thy wonderful works which thou hast done, and thy thoughts which are to us-ward: they cannot be reckoned up in order unto thee: if I would declare and speak of them, they are more than can be numbered.*" Lively and vital worship is always a response to the mighty works of God in history and human experience. The more aware we are of God's goodness and grace, the more unrestrained and joyful our worship.

The Psalmist not only praised God, he witnessed to God, told everybody what God had done for him. Some would be impressed, others embarrassed. There are people who never talk about their religion because they consider it in bad form, a disclosure of their own privacy and an invasion of the rights of others. Yet those very people, if a noted surgeon operated on them and saved them from death, would be quick to praise him and recommend him to their friends. That's what the Psalmist did with God. He even went to church and preached a sermon. *"I have preached righteousness in the great congregation: lo, I have not refrained my lips, O Lord, thou knowest. I have not hid thy righteousness within my heart; I have declared thy faithfulness and thy salvation . . ."* To be sure, a person will not talk about his religion when he has nothing to say; but when God has acted in his life with grace and power, how can he keep silent?

The Psalmist made another response to God's goodness. His words suggest that it was customary to purchase an animal and present it for sacrifice as a tangible thank-offering to God for mercies received. In a token sense that is still a custom in every service of worship. We present an offering of money after the sermon as our response to the Word of God, not the word spoken by the preacher but the Incarnate Word to which the spoken word bears witness. Sometimes a thank-offering may be large and substantial. Many have been the buildings, bequests, endowments and scholarships given as memorials of people who died. The 40th Psalm is the memorial of a person who lived. In his illness he vowed that if God healed him he would build a church or endow a theological college or send a gift of money to the mission field. He kept his vow. That was his response.

But it was not enough. The Psalmist, perhaps as he meditated in the temple, suddenly realised that worship, witness and generosity, though eminently pleasing to God, are not the response that God wants. In fact, it is possible to worship God exquisitely, witness to him eloquently and contribute to him liberally, yet still withhold the response that God wants. It is even possible that God does *not* want our prayer and praise and substance, if that's all we have to give him. So declared the Psalmist: *"Sacrifice and offering thou didst not desire . . . burnt offer-*

ing and sin offering hast thou not required." Actually God wants
nothing the worshipper can give, he wants the worshipper
himself. The acceptable offering is a self-offering, a complete
and total commitment to obey God's will. That is what the
Psalmist gave: "*Then said I, Lo I come: in the volume of the book it is
written of me, I delight to do thy will, O my God . . .*"

Louis Evans tells the beautiful story of an old Indian chief
who made that response to the Gospel. In gratitude for his
new-found faith and joy he came to the missionary bearing in
his hands a pair of beaded moccasins. "Me give these to Jesus,"
he said. But the missionary shook his head and replied, "No
chief, that is not what Jesus wants." Bewildered, he took them
back to his teepee and this time brought some finely-woven
snowshoes. "No", said the missionary, "that is not what Jesus
wants." Finally he went and got his most precious treasure, a
well-oiled automatic rifle. Surely that would be accepted. But
the missionary said, "No chief, that is not what Jesus wants."
The old man stood there, puzzled, not knowing what to do next.
Then, as though a light had dawned, he lifted his eyes and said,
"Well, then, me give Jesus poor Indian too." The missionary
smiled and said, "Yes chief, it is you yourself that Jesus wants,
and nothing less will do."[1]

That is the great lesson of the 40th Psalm. It tells us that
before we give God our worship, our witness and our money we
must give him ourselves and say with the Psalmist, "I delight to
do thy will, O my God." That is the response that God wants to
his Gospel. Nothing less will do. It might be said that obedience
to God's will is the basic principle of the religious life, even
more basic than love. A few years ago the proponents of situation ethics were trying to reduce all religion to love. They said
that there are no rules in Christianity except love and that in
any situation the Christian may decide what's right by simply
asking one question. "What is the loving thing to do?" A
Christian does ask that question but he asks it second. First he
asks, "What is the will of God in this situation?" A Christian is
supremely a person committed to do the will of God. That is his
response to the Gospel. Always his prayers include a prayer of
obedience, "I delight to do thy will, O my God."

A Christian writer in the New Testament puts those very
words into the mouth of Jesus; and it is possible that Jesus said

them, he whose mind was saturated in the Psalms and who quoted them even on the Cross. Writing of the Jewish sacrificial system, the author of the Epistle to the Hebrews tells how the animal sacrifices of the old covenant have been abolished by the one perfect sacrifice of Christ on his Cross. Yet it was not the offer of his body to be killed that constituted his perfect sacrifice but the commitment of his will to the will of God. "Then said he, Lo, I come to do thy will, O God." (Heb 10:9 AV) At the beginning of his ministry he told the disciples, "My meat is to do the will of him that sent me, and to finish his work." (John 4:34 AV) At the end, after he had prayed that the Cross would be removed from him, he said to God, "Nevertheless not my will, but thine, be done." (Luke 22:42 AV) He who came not only to reveal God but to reveal man showed us that human life at its highest and best is life completely committed to obey the will of God.

The 40th Psalm makes it plain, however, that such commitment can only be our response to a saving experience of God. We hear complaints these days that the mainline churches, despite their modern methods, are losing ground because their members are not committed. We hear also and read books to the effect that the conservative churches, without the help of gimmicks, are growing because their members *are* committed. In the former case it is true that the parish roll of many a church today is padded with the names of people who feel no commitment to support it or share in its work or even attend services. Those same people have a strong sense of commitment to their work, their families and their own pleasure. Why not to God? The answer is that such commitment cannot be self-generated; it can only be a response to the Gospel.

Not only the Gospel but a personal experience of the Gospel. It is not enough simply to rehearse the mighty acts of God as if one were rehearsing a list of military victories. The Psalmist had been doing that all his life. He knew that God had created the world and provided for his people and delivered them from slavery in Egypt. It was when God, who had created and provided for him, delivered *him* from slavery that he could respond with an act of total commitment, "I delight to do thy will, O my God." It is not enough for a Christian, year after year and in every service of Holy Communion, to celebrate the great drama of redemption in the birth, life, ministry, death, resurrection and ascension of Christ. He must appropriate those acts of God in a personal way. He must make the Gospel his own. Then he can respond to it.

So it happened to Nicholas Ludwig, Count of Zinzendorf, who came one afternoon to a famous chapel in Europe where he noticed a celebrated picture of Jesus on the Cross. It was said that the artist had experienced so deeply the saving power of the Cross in his life that when he came to paint a likeness of his Lord, his soul was filled with tenderest love, and he painted love into every feature. The young nobleman was fascinated by it. He saw love in the pierced hands, love in the bleeding brow, love in the wounded side. Slowly he scanned the couplet which the artist had written at the base of the painting, as though spoken by Christ: "All this I did for thee, What hast thou done for me?" Late that afternoon, as the rays of the setting sun slanted through the stained-glass window, they fell on a bowed figure weeping and sobbing his commitment to the Christ whose love had not only saved his soul but conquered his heart. From that day the service of Christ claimed him completely, and he expressed his devotion by writing some great hymns of praise.

> Jesus, thy blood and righteousness
> My beauty are, my glorious dress;
> 'Midst flaming worlds, in these arrayed,
> With joy I shall lift up my head.

The writer of those lines gave everything to the God who had given everything to him. He gave himself. He made the only response that any person can make before the Cross of Christ: "*I delight to do thy will, O my God.*"

NOTES TO PSALM 40

1. Louis Evans, *Youth Seeks a Master* (Fleming H. Revell Company, New York, 1941) pp. 97–98.

Psalm 42

He Feels Despondent

One of the most distinguished novels in recent years is a book entitled *Roots*.[1] The author, Alex Haley, traced his ancestral roots to a man whose African name was Kunta Kinte. Mr. Haley went to Africa and visited the tribe from which Kunta came and there he reconstructed the story of the youth growing up among a people whose culture and civilisation were remarkably advanced. They educated their children, had strong family loyalties and stern moral standards and were devout Muslims. In 1767 slave traders captured the young man as they would capture a wild animal and transported him to America where he was enslaved and treated like a wild animal. In that foreign land his enemies taunted and brutalised him. Several times he tried to escape and was finally punished by having the front part of his foot chopped off with an axe. No one could get through to him for a long time. He became sullen, withdrawn and despondent. He longed for his home and his God. He tried to pray, but God seemed very far away.

The author of Psalms 42 and 43, which originally were a single piece, felt despondent for much the same reason. He too was separated from his country and therefore felt separated from his God. Wistfully he recalls the sheer joy of worshipping God in the temple, and his soul thirsts for God as a wild animal thirsts for water when overtaken by hunters or by drought. "*As the hart panteth after the water brooks, so panteth my soul after thee, O God. My soul thirsteth for God, for the living God: when shall I come and appear before God?*" Now, instead of the joyous temple music, he is deafened by the thunder of waterfalls and mountain torrents as "*deep calleth unto deep at the noise of they waterspouts*". They seem to symbolise his calamities; and he calls them God's "*waves and billows which are gone over me*". The scoffing of the heathen deepens his despondency. They are idolaters, worshipping gods which they can see and touch, ridiculing him for his simple faith in the living God who seems invisible and indifferent and far away. Their mockery feels like a mortal wound in his body, and their derisive question, "*Where is thy God?*" reduces him to tears and becomes the question of his own tortured soul.

Devout believers have often asked themselves that question, and many are asking it now. They feel exiled in a foreign country, or a foreign century, where the very language and customs are strange to them and where all the old familiar landmarks are gone. They feel lost in a secular society where churches are empty and sports stadiums filled, where modern idolaters have turned from the living God to worship the gods of money, pleasure, science and sex that they can see and hear and touch. From all sides comes the piercing question, "Where is thy God? Why doesn't he show himself, if he exists at all? Why doesn't he save you from your troubles and why doesn't he do something about the tragedy of the world?" That becomes our question too. Sometimes it makes us feel despondent. We may even shed tears.

The Psalmist, however, did more than torture himself by asking, "Where is thy God?" He reacted to the absent God in a positive and constructive way and in so doing dealt with his despondency. Stage by stage he raised himself from the depths of despair to fullness of trust and peace of soul. Any devout person who feels despondent for the same reason can well afford to imitate his pattern of behaviour. Actually he looked in three directions—past, present and future.

First, he looked to the past. He searched the archives of his memory and brought out pictures of the great religious festivals. "*When I remember these things, I pour out my soul in me: for I had gone with the multitude, I went with them to the house of God, with the voice of joy and praise, with a multitude that kept holyday.*" That memory steadied and heartened him. He might question his own soul, but the affirmation of the multitude could not be denied.

The lesson of the 42nd Psalm is that the spiritual life has its low moods and its high moods. Much of the time we live on the lower level, but occasionally there comes a rare and luminous experience unlike anything we have ever known before. Under its inspiration we think thoughts that we have never thought before, we dream dreams that we have never dreamed before, we believe ourselves capable of achievements that would normally seem impossible. In that high hour it is as though all heaven were open about us and we could reach out our hand and touch the hand of God. The Psalm is telling us to trust those high moods and preserve them in our memory like photographs to be taken out and looked at on days when clouds cover the sky and God seems far away.

There was a man whose hobby had been mountain climbing and who decorated his office wall with framed photographs of the peaks he had scaled and the views he had caught. He told visitors, "Whenever things get impossible around the office, I take a few minutes off to glance at those pictures, remembering with each scene how it looked from there." That's what the Psalmist did. In the valley of despondency he brought out pictures of the spiritual mountain tops and remembered the way that things looked from there. He compared the glorious past to the dismal present and said to himself, "That was the truth, not this."

In looking back as he did, the Psalmist typified one of the finest instincts of his people. They had a great instinct for history. Their God was the God of history. Whenever they felt despondent they looked back into history, they held a consultation with the past, and it brought them through the miseries of the present. Again and again the Psalmists, Prophets and Lawgivers of the Old Testament comforted their people and wiped away their tears by rehearsing the mighty acts of God in history, his acts of Creation, Providence and Redemption. "Remember the former things of old; for I am God, and there is no other; I am God, and there is none like me . . . look to the rock from which you were hewn, and to the quarry from which you were digged." (Isa 46:9;51:1 RSV)

Emerson caught that spirit when he said, "Let the hours be silent so that the centuries may speak." That was said also by another person in a different way. On one of the streets of

London there is a church with pealing bells that carry their music across the city. Nearby is a tall, modern building, the headquarters of a daily newspaper. When some of the employees complained to the Vicar that his bells annoyed them, he retorted, "We have been here eight hundred years. How long have you been here?" The newspaper has since gone out of business, and the church is still there. That's something to remember in these days of rapidly-changing headlines when nothing in our personal and corporate lives seems stable any more. Our God is the God of the centuries. He called Abraham to be the father of a new people, gave Moses the Ten Commandments, spoke through the prophets, came to live with us in Jesus, raised Jesus from the dead, sent his Holy Spirit on the church, and has guided and protected his people through nineteen turbulent centuries. How can we ask, "Where is *that* God?"

As a second stage in dealing with despondency the Psalmist looked at the present. Actually he looked at himself. In fact, he talked to himself and rebuked himself. *"Why art thou cast down, O my soul? and why art thou disquieted within me?"* It's a good thing a psychiatrist didn't come along and interrupt him, else he might have been made to feel like an eccentric.

There is nothing eccentric about talking to yourself. Shakespeare's characters do it all the time; their most famous speeches are their soliloquies. Soliloquy can be a helpful form of self-analysis, a means of lifting yourself out of your depressed moods. "So I feel spiritually down. Why? Am I suffering pain or nervous tension or passing through a personal crisis? Those are common causes of spiritual depression, but once they have been dealt with, I needn't feel depressed any more." The Psalmist was having his troubles. He felt homesick and physically ill and beaten down by the taunts of his enemies. That didn't mean that God had deserted him. It didn't really justify the question, "Where is thy God?"

Yet people have always asked that question; it has literally sobbed its way down the centuries. Whenever their own sufferings or the sufferings of the world crush their spirits, they cry out plaintively or angrily, "Where is God? Does he know? Does he care?" The answer, of course, is that God does know and

does care, because he has been in it too. He was in the gentlest
man who ever lived and was crucified for it, the kindest friend
anyone ever had and was betrayed for it with thirty pieces of
silver clinking coldly in a leather bag. God has been in the midst
of all human tears. He lost his Son there. If someone asks,
"Where is God today?", the answer is that God is suffering with
us, suffering the agony of a love offered and rejected. He stands
in hospitals beside every bed of pain, in prison cells beside every
victim of racial injustice, in city streets beside every starving
child. God is wherever there is sorrow and suffering and poverty and heartbreak. The prophet said of old, "In all their
affliction he was afflicted." (Isa 63:9 AV)

God not only suffers with us, he not only knows and cares, he
acts redemptively on our behalf. God is very active in the world
today, and we shall see signs of his activity if we look around us
through the eyes of faith. The heroism and devotion of Christian missionaries in hostile countries; the relief of human suffering being administered by national and international social
agencies; the protest against racial and religious bigotry from
people who are able to think straightly and feel humanely; the
championship of intellectual freedom and civil liberties by
distinguished scientists, courageous educators and selfless
politicians; the fresh, valiant, creative thinking which has been
done and is still being done with respect to the abolition of
poverty and war; the faith, fidelity and devotion to be found in
the best of our churches—are all signs of God's activity and
they fill us not with dismay but with confidence and hope. How
can we ask today, "Where is thy God?"

How can we ever ask that question, which is really a question
of mankind's childhood? It assumes that if God is here he is not
there, if he is there he is not here. That's what the Psalmist
assumed at first. If he had answered his enemies who scoffed
and asked, "Where is thy God?" he would probably have said,
"In the temple at Jerusalem." The more deeply he thought
about it, however, the more he realised that God is everywhere—not only in Jerusalem but in Jordan and Mount Her-
mon, not only in the temple but in the marketplace, not only in
the sunshine but in the storm, not only in the flower but in the
earthquake, not only in victory but in defeat, not only in
laughter but in tears. Wherever a person stands on the earth's

surface or in this vast universe, he stands in the presence of God. The world does not contain God; rather, God contains the world and the whole creation. Therefore, he is everywhere. The scoffers may not see him, though they cannot escape him; but the person of faith will see him. "Why art thou cast down, O my soul? and why art thou disquieted within me?"

Having looked to the past and present, the Psalmist looked also to the future. Three times he asked his soul, *"Why art thou cast down?"* and each time said to his soul, *"Hope thou in God: for I shall yet praise him, who is the health of my countenance, and my God."* Hope, as a creative way of looking at the future, does hold the secret of health; it can make all the difference between life and death.

Viktor Frankl, the psychiatrist, writing from his experience as an inmate in a concentration camp, tells that hope was the one thing that kept the prisoners alive. They might lose their freedom and dignity, but as long as they kept their hope they survived. When they lost hope they were doomed. He tells how the death rate increased dramatically between Christmas and New Year at the end of 1944. The cause did not lie in harder working conditions or inadequate food or change of weather or new epidemics. It was simply that the majority of prisoners had been kept alive by the naive hope that they would be home again by Christmas. When Christmas came and went, they lost hope. That lowered their powers of resistance, and a great number of them died.[2]

Even a limited hope can restore health to one's countenance, for God may fulfil that hope in a larger sense than we expect. In effect, the Psalmist hoped that the absent God would come to him again and lead him from the darkness of doubt into the glorious light of faith. Such was the blessing granted to the Apostle Thomas who was not present in the upper room on Easter Day. The death of Jesus had plunged him into the deepest gloom, and it was a gloom unrelieved by the exuberance of the other disciples who told him that they had seen their risen Lord. Thomas could only reply, "Unless I see . . . I will not believe." A week later the risen Christ came again to the upper room and showed that doubting disciple the wounds in his hands and side. His doubt dispelled forever, Thomas cried

out in exultant devotion, "My Lord and my God!" (John
20:24–27 RSV) That little drama confirms our hope that God
will never leave us in the darkness of doubt but will come to us
and lead us into the light of renewed praise.

There was a larger sense in which the Psalmist hoped in God,
a sense that helped him to deal with the taunts of his enemies.
He hoped that in time God would vindicate him and deal with
his enemies. That was the hope of a Christian in Germany who
said that he survived the Hitler regime because behind all the
shrieking oratory and marching feet and clashing weapons he
could hear the ticking of an eternal clock. He believed that
Hitler's time was running out, God would drop the curtain on
Hitler, and scoffers would no longer ask, "Where is thy God?"
Such was the hope of the Psalmist—not optimism, not wishful
thinking, but a mighty exercise of trust in God, in his love, his
purpose, his power, his control of human life and history. Ask
him how he could express such trust and confidence just when
he felt that God had deserted him, and he might have given a
somewhat illogical answer.

Christians, however, need not give an illogical answer. They
know why they place their hope in God. Paul states the reason
in his Letter to the Ephesians: "He has made known to us his
hidden purpose . . . namely, that the universe, all in heaven and
on earth, might be brought into a unity in Christ." (Eph 1:9–10
NEB) In that view history does not go around in circles but
moves toward a goal, God's goal. God has a purpose for history
which he revealed in the perfect obedience of Jesus. In God's
purpose the whole creation is moving toward that perfect
obedience, and in that sense Jesus himself is a preview of the
end of history. God's purpose can never be defeated. It may be
thwarted by crucifixions along the way but it will rise above
them and ultimately prevail; and the universe, all in heaven
and on earth, will be brought into a unity in Christ. In its very
largest sense that is what a Christian means when he says to his
soul, "Hope thou in God: for I shall yet praise him, who is the
health of my countenance, and my God."

NOTES TO PSALM 42

1. Published by Dell Publishing Co., Inc., New York, 1977.
2. Viktor Frankl, *Man's Search for Meaning* (Hodder and Stoughton, London, 1964).

Psalm 48

He Feels Proud

The prevailing mood of the 48th Psalm is one of unfettered pride. The Psalmist sings about Jerusalem and he sings with patriotism and love. That is his reaction not only to Jerusalem itself and its glorious history but to the presence of God and to God's care and protection of the holy city. His words expressed the feelings of all the worshippers of God toward the city where God dwelt. They became a hymn of praise on the lips of pilgrims who journeyed through deserts and across seas to join in the sacred festivals.

There have been two occasions when the words of the 48th Psalm came tumbling into my mind. I sensed the spirit of the Psalmist the first time I caught a glimpse of the Holy City. It was in 1962 when I guided a pilgrimage of Christian people through the lands of the Bible. We started in Galilee, then drove south along the Mediterranean coast to Tel Aviv, and from there went inland. Suddenly in the distance we saw Jerusalem high on a hill. "Stop the bus!" I shouted, much to the driver's consternation. He pulled over to the side of the road, and we became a worshipping congregation as we opened our Bibles and read in unison the familiar words, *"Beautiful for situation, the joy of the whole earth, is Mount Zion, on the sides of the north, the city of the great King."* Spiritually we were preparing ourselves to enter the beautiful city; and God seemed to be saying to us, as he said to his pilgrims long ago, *"Walk about Zion, and go round about her: tell the towers thereof. Mark ye well her bulwarks, consider her palaces; that ye may tell it to the generation following."*

Again I thought of the 48th Psalm when I saw a fascinating film that was produced as part of the campaign for the restoration of Canterbury Cathedral. Prince Charles is the star of the film. With him we walk about Zion and go round about her. We stand in the chancel and listen to the exquisite choir, we rest in the cloisters and talk with the Archbishop of Canterbury, we pause at the tombs of kings, we see the place where Beckett was martyred, we ascend the stone steps worn down by the feet of Canterbury pilgrims. With Charles we tell the towers thereof. He takes us up in the towers and shows us the incomparable stonework that was fashioned by the hands of dedicated craftsmen. We mark well her bulwarks, the walls, foundations and buttresses that have stood the storms of fourteen centuries. We consider her palaces as we join the worshipping congregation and listen to the young Prince read a lesson from Proverbs. The whole film tells the story of historic Canterbury to a new generation. "Tell it to the generation following."

Christians are proud of Jerusalem and Canterbury, yet their most sacred pride is directed not to a single city or to a single building but to the whole structure of God's church on earth. In that sense they share the reaction of the Psalmist, and in that larger figurative sense we shall interpret the 48th Psalm.

"Walk about Zion, and go round about her . . ." That's what Christians need to do if they want to recover their love for the church, their sense of pride in the church. Some never do that. They are like invalids confined to their own bedrooms who never see the rest of the house; like people who live in a city suburb and have never seen other suburbs, never been downtown, never travelled into the country, never visited other cities. They stay put in their own small corner of the church and never venture beyond it. They never worship in any church building but their own, not even when they are on holiday. They don't know how vast and varied the whole church of God is. They think, or behave as though they think, that the limits of God's Kingdom ends with the limits of their own parish.

That is an insular attitude and it can be destructive especially if the local church falls on bad times. The value of ranging over the whole church is that we can see our own congregation as part of a total picture, and that gives us a healthy realism. A magazine article entitled "Can the Churches Survive?" told of the dwindling resources of once-great churches in the changing areas of American cities—how some are being forced to close, others to amalgamate, and how others are meeting the challenge with new and exciting forms of ministry. Such an article should be compulsory reading for laymen in positions of local church leadership. Before they begin blaming the clergy or the choristers or the Christian education programmes for the current decline in membership and finances, let them walk about Zion and get an accurate sociological picture of the total situation.

On the other hand, a walk about Zion may quicken their sense of pride in belonging to a very large family. They will discover that although the church has fallen back in some parts of the world, yet in other parts it is moving ahead by leaps and bounds. In Africa, to which we were sending missionaries a few years ago, church membership is increasing by nearly six percent a year, more than twice the continent's birthrate; and it is estimated that by the close of the century 355 million believers, fully half the continent, may be Christian. "If this happens", says one church leader, "it will make Africa the centre of world Christianity." Presbyterians in Taiwan celebrated the 100th Anniversary of the arrival of missionaries in their country with a ten-year programme to double the number of churches and the total membership in all churches. They succeeded beyond all expectations. Those are encouraging facts, and they are facts about the whole family of God to which Christians belong. We need never be ashamed of the church because of what we see in a single congregation or a single country. If we let our minds range across history and throughout the world, if we "walk about Zion, and go round about her", we shall be proud of the church.

"Tell the towers thereof . . ." Two different magazines recently published articles which asked the same question: Where are the great men today? In each case the journalist expressed concern that in all areas of life we are not producing the heroes, the leaders, the towering men and women of a generation ago. Indeed, our culture seems almost to discourage qualities of leadership. Educational systems cater to the average mind and

force all students into the same mould of mediocrity. Politics, labour unions, business, industry, the arts and the media promote a monotonous egalitarianism. A comic cartoon shows a father and son walking down a city street and looking at an unusual statue—a group of stone figures huddled together on a stone pedestal. The father is saying, "You see, my boy, there are no more great men, only great committees." That could be one reason why some Christians have lost their sense of pride in the church. They can tell the committees but not the towers thereof.

Nevertheless, the church has its towers, its tall people, outstanding men and women who rise above the rest of us. God has raised them up in every generation, else the church would have gone defunct a long time ago. It might be a good idea to hang their portraits in a picture gallery, even in a literal sense. For example, I have in my study a photograph of two elderly men looking at each other with the light of reconciliation in their eyes. They are Professor Karl Barth and Professor Emil Brunner, two of the greatest theologians of this century and of all the centuries. They taught in the neighbouring Swiss cities of Basel and Zurich, but their communications broke down because their theologies separated them years ago. At last they were brought together by an American missionary to Japan, Dr. John Hesselink, who is now a Seminary President in Michigan. He took the photograph and gave me a copy of it. Two theological giants, intellectual towers of the church in our generation! Let us hang their portraits in our picture gallery of saints alongside the great men and women of the church in every generation. Let us step inside the gallery occasionally and look at those portraits, let us "tell the towers thereof", and we shall be proud of the church.

"*Mark ye well her bulwarks . . .*" In the Psalm, that refers to the defence structures of Jerusalem. They are not as impressive as the towers but they are just as important, perhaps more so. You can do without towers but you can't do without bulwarks. They keep the city strong and secure, they hold off invaders. The towers might fall if it were not for the bulwarks. Neither are the church's bulwarks all that impressive or even that noticeable, but we should notice them quickly enough if they were suddenly removed. They are the strong defenders of the church, the servants of the church, the quiet people who by their love, their loyalty and their devotion hold up its structures.

There have been bulwarks in every congregation that I have been privileged to serve. They were not always the articulate leaders; often they were people who remained in the background and had very little to say; but they were the workers. There was a farmer in my first rural parish who didn't have much to say because he stuttered badly and took all evening to get out a single sentence. One evening at a congregational meeting he got out a very pregnant sentence. We had been discussing a pre-digested stewardship campaign to raise more money for denominational funds when this man surprised us by saying, "You can count me out. I already give forty percent of my cash income to the church." He didn't stutter when he said that. He was a bulwark of the church, as are all people who support it with their substance and attend its worship regularly and sing in the choir and teach Sunday School and canvass for money and serve in the organisations and spare no effort to promote its spirit of harmony and peace. When others forsake the church, as people once forsook Jesus, so that he asked the disciples, "Will you also go away?", they reply with Peter, "To whom shall we go? You have the words of eternal life." (John 6:67,68 RSV) Those are the church's bulwarks. If we mark them well we shall be proud of the church.

"*Consider her palaces* ..." We are back to Canterbury Cathedral, because a cathedral compared to a parish church is like Buckingham Palace compared to a modest home. Consider the palaces, the great cathedrals of Britain and Europe—spacious, magnificent houses of worship set in the midst of busy cities and dedicated to the life of the soul and the service of faith. Just to be inside one of them is an experience of worship. The very arches and pillars, the glorious stained glass, the exquisite sculpture, the vaulted ceiling and the mighty organ, all bequeathed by the vision, the faith, the generosity and the zeal of past generations, point us upwards to the glory of God.

Yet we know that stones and sculpture and marble floors and stained glass windows are not the materials that comprise the most enduring palaces which the church has built through the centuries. The great palaces, especially those being built today, are fashioned with human materials. You will see many of them if you travel through the developing countries of Asia and Africa. When Angola gained her independence, and white people were beginning to leave that troubled country, a Canadian medical missionary sent his family home and insisted on remaining there himself because he was the only qualified doctor in charge of five mission hospitals. Consider those five palaces and alongside them set the schools and agricultural institutes which have raised the level of human life and given people a sense of dignity and selfhood. At home take a look at the programmes of community outreach in the downtown areas of cities. See what the church is doing for the poor and needy, the senior citizens, and the delinquent and disadvantaged members of society. See what the church is doing in and through the lives of its people. Those palaces of human service will endure when all our material structures have become archaeological ruins. Let us consider them and we shall be proud of the church.

"Walk about Zion . . . that ye may tell it to the generation following." Prince Charles does that in the film. He walks about historic Canterbury and tells the younger generation, his own generation, what the great cathedral means to him. He says, "Every time I come here I find something new and even more beautiful which has escaped my notice before . . . The very nature of the place is to raise men's eyes and men's minds to greater things; to things of eternity and peace and beauty." That is what Charles says to our children about Canterbury. What shall we say to them about the church?

We shall not speak cynically as do some modern church historians who write in a debunking manner and employ a kind of clever trick-writing to ingratiate themselves with their unchurched contemporaries. They say, in effect, "You think that the church is rotten. Let us tell you how rotten it really is. Its money is invested in human exploitation. Its leaders are all megalomaniacs. Its missions are responsible for East-West tension today. Its Gospel promotes race prejudice." Lies and half-truths, to be sure, but the whole cultural climate is shot through with them. Newspapers, books, radio, television, theatre, teachers, parents, friends and even Christians continually run down the church to our children. Surely our children need to get the picture in its right perspective. Surely they need to be told the truth about the church, the whole truth, not only about its weaknesses but about its strength, not only about its failures but about its accomplishments, not only about its defeats but about its victories.

Some years ago a newspaper in Britain offered a prize for the best essay on the subject, "What is wrong with the church?" There were plenty of entries, because plenty of people were prepared and are still prepared to answer that question at great length. In fact, they will answer it without being asked. The prize was won by a clergyman from Wales who gave this answer: "What is wrong with the church is our failure to realise and wonder at the beauty, the mystery, the glory and the greatness of the church." We need to walk about Zion, and go round about her. We need to tell the towers thereof. We need to mark well her bulwarks and consider her palaces. We need to tell it to the generation following. Let us do that, and we shall be proud of the church.

Psalm 73

He Feels Rewarded

There was a man who became bitter for a while after the death of his son. He was a boy of whom any parents could be proud. He worked hard in school, got excellent grades, played a trumpet in the school band. He was a perfect gentleman, popular with his friends, loving toward his family, devoted to the church. At age sixteen he developed cancer and died after a painful struggle. The father, a quiet man, said with strange intensity, "Why did it have to be my son? He was such a good boy. He never hurt anyone in his life. Look at those motorcycle maniacs tearing up and down the street. Why could it not have been one of them? There is no justice in the world. I feel like becoming an atheist. How can I believe in a good God?"

That is a problem as old as the human race and as modern as yesterday's newspaper. People have grappled with it from the beginning of time. It can be stated simply: why do the righteous suffer and the wicked prosper? Why does the good person so often get the stick while the bad person gets the pie? How can we believe that a just God created and governs a world that seems so utterly indifferent to moral values?

Never did anyone grapple more passionately with that problem than did the writer of the 73rd Psalm. He reacted to his experience of God in two ways: first he felt cheated, then he felt rewarded; and the Psalm is the story of his transition from one to the other. As a devout Jew he had grown up with an inherited belief in the justice of God. He states his belief:

> *Truly God is good to the upright,*
> *to those who are pure in heart.*[1]

That's a comforting belief—"Be good, and God will be good to you." But what if it doesn't work out? What if you are good, and God isn't good to you but is good to bad people? Then you will feel cheated as the Psalmist felt cheated. In fact, the hard blows of life nearly knocked him off his feet.

> *But as for me, my feet had almost stumbled,*
> *my steps had well nigh slipped.*

Tradition identifies the author of Psalm 73 as Asaph, a brilliant poet and musician of his generation. His name doesn't matter, though, because Asaph is every man in every genera-tion whose structure of faith groans and totters under the pressure of hard facts and grim reality. He speaks for many people when he says,

> *For I was envious of the arrogant,*
> *when I saw the prosperity of the wicked.*
> *They are not in trouble as other men are;*
> *they are not stricken like other men.*

From where he sat it looked to Asaph as if there were no justice in the world, no moral order, no order at all. As he saw it, a man could be ruthless, selfish, materialistic and immoral, he could be all kinds of a devil and get away scot free. Obviously it did no good to obey God and keep the commandments. *He* had been obedient, *he* had been virtuous, *he* had been devout, and *he* had been kicked all over the place like a dog ill-treated by its master.

> *All in vain have I kept my heart clean*
> *and washed my hands in innocence.*
> *For all the day long I have been stricken,*
> *and chastened every morning.*

We can admire Asaph for a number of reasons, chiefly the constructive way in which he handled his spiritual difficulty. To begin with, he kept quiet about his problem, he chose to work it out by himself instead of loading it on other people and making it their problem too. Why do some people, when their faith begins cracking, shout it aloud from the housetops or the television screen and clamour to get it into print, foisting their doubts like a grudge upon the rising generation? If they can't believe, they will make sure, by heaven, that nobody else can either! An impulse of that kind may have tempted the Psalmist, but something checked him:

> *If I had said, "I will speak thus",*
> *I would have been untrue to the*
> *generation of thy children.*

Asaph pictured his disillusionment becoming universal. He saw an entire generation growing up bereft of ideals, without any spiritual consciousness, living for material ends alone; and the very thought of it seized him with a sickening horror. What a disgusting and dreadful hell this earth would be if it were populated by a race wholly destitute of faith in God! Struggle with doubt himself? Yes. But to bear on his conscience the guilt of infecting with that doubt the impressionable boys and girls in his home, his school, his community? He could not be so inhuman, so cruel.

We can admire Asaph for another reason. Many a person, disillusioned about God, becomes cynical. He stops going to church, puts on the pose of an agnostic and flings away from religion altogether—which is an unwise thing to do, because he cuts himself off from the spiritual resources which in the end might resolve his doubts and restore his faith. If Asaph felt tempted to become a cynic, his fine soul resisted the temptation. Wearied with the struggle, he did the wisest thing that any person can do. He turned to religion with a new earnestness, re-examined his beliefs with a new seriousness, went to church with a new humility and saw his problem in a new perspective.

> *But when I thought how to understand this,*
> *it seemed to me a wearisome task,*
> *until I went into the sanctuary of God.*

In "the sanctuary of God", a phrase that may describe a sacred building or a reverent mind, certain great truths became very clear to the writer of the 73rd Psalm.

First, he saw how illusory is the prosperity of the wicked. Out in the world, where people think only in terms of human, materialistic values, it looked as though evil, instead of being penalised, actually paid off. Proud, violent, conceited, impious men enjoyed the reward promised to the righteous—prosperity, strength, peace in life and in death. But how different it all appeared inside the sanctuary. There in the atmosphere of eternal values the Psalmist could say to God concerning the wicked,

> . . . then I perceived their end.
> Truly thou dost set them in slippery places;
> thou dost make them fall to ruin.
> How they are destroyed in a moment,
> swept away utterly by terrors!
> They are like a dream when one awakes,
> on awaking you despise their phantoms.

That was no wishful thinking on Asaph's part, because now he saw one truth above all else. He saw that evil, no matter how successful it appears in terms of wealth and power, is still evil at all times, in all places and in all people. He saw that in God's world God always answers the evil-doer, and it is a full answer given in God's own time and way.

The most dramatic illustration of that truth in the Bible is Isaiah's Oracle on the Death of the King of Babylon. (Isa 14:1-21 RSV) It is like a drama which takes place on two levels. Scene One shows a picture of earth rejoicing in its freedom from the hated tyrant. "The whole earth is at rest and quiet; they break forth into singing." Scene Two takes us down to Sheol, the dusty prison house of the ghostly dead, where the spectres of discredited kings greet the new arrival. "You too have become weak as we! You have become like us!" In Scene Three, still in Sheol, we hear heaven's thunderous accusation against this human titan who tried to make himself equal to God and has now been cast aside like an unclean thing to the derisive laughter of the God he mocked. Scene Four, back on earth, shows the incredulity of people as they gaze at the defaced image of the dictator, a mood that was surely felt at the infamous deaths of Hitler and Mussolini. "Is this the man . . . who made the world like a desert and overthrew its cities, who did not let his prisoners go home?" It is a commentary in the 73rd Psalm, ". . . then I perceived their end. Truly thou dost set them in slippery places; thou dost make them fall to ruin".

A second truth that laid hold of the Psalmist, as he brooded over life in the sanctuary, was the truth of his own ignorance and blasphemy. Like all devout Jews he believed the too-simple theory that God should reward righteousness and punish wickedness, but now for the first time he examined the implications of that theory. Suppose it worked like a computer? Suppose piety did always issue in prosperity and sin in suffering? Wouldn't that deprive God of any personal judgment? Would it not make virtue prudential rather than moral, and goodness a kind of insurance policy taken out by shrewd, calculating moralists for the sake of saving their own skins?

The Psalmist did a sensible thing in the sanctuary: he forgot about the evil-doers and took a good look at himself. In effect, he asked himself, "How do I know that I am one of the righteous? Since when did God delegate to me or to any person the right to decide who is righteous and who is wicked, the right to administer Divine punishments and rewards?" In the sanctuary Asaph saw himself for what he was—a child quarrelling with his father because the parent had not disciplined the family according to his childish conceptions of justice; worse than a child—an animal expecting from his master a piece of meat for his tricks and a kick for having fouled the household furniture. With shame he poured out his confession:

> *When my soul was embittered,*
> *when I was pricked in heart,*
> *I was stupid and ignorant,*
> *I was like a beast toward thee.*

Suppose God did deal justly with us? Suppose he gave us exactly what our goodness deserves? Suppose he judged us by his own laws, the Ten Commandments? (Exodus 20:1ff AV) How should we measure up to them? "Thou shalt have no other gods before me"—How high does God rate in our list of priorities? "Thou shalt not make unto thee any graven image"—Have we never tried to cut God down to our own size? "Thou shalt not take the name of the Lord thy God in vain"—Do we always speak God's name with complete sincerity? "Thou shalt not kill"—Jesus said that anger kills. "Thou shalt not commit adultery"—Jesus said that we do it in our hearts. Judged by those laws and the Beatitudes and the teachings of Paul and the moral wisdom of the centuries, we may not come off very well. In fact, we may even realise, as the

Psalmist did, that it's a good thing that God does not deal justly with us but rather shows kindness and mercy.

In the quiet of the sanctuary Asaph learned another truth. He learned that God does reward goodness—not with material favours but with something more precious. To the good man, the righteous man, the godly man, God gives what he can never give to the ungodly: he gives himself. He does not exempt a good person from the sufferings which are common to all humanity but he does give him a transforming presence that saves his suffering from bitterness and defeat. That was enough for Asaph, more than enough. His feeling changed from being cheated to being rewarded, and he prayed from a heart overflowing with gratitude,

> *Nevertheless I am continually with thee;*
>   *thou dost hold my right hand.*
> *Thou dost guide me with thy counsel,*
>   *and afterward thou wilt receive me to glory.*

The Psalmist sees four rewards of a good man—first, a sense of *God's companionship*; and that is a blessed gift in a world where so many people are lost in loneliness and despair. It was the reward of the elder brother in Jesus' parable of the Prodigal Son. That faithful fellow resented the fuss made over the penitent prodigal while he, who had dutifully stayed at home and served his father, received no recognition whatever. When he complained bitterly, his father lovingly replied, "Son, you are always with me . . ." (Luke 15:31 RSV). That was the reward denied to the young rebel whose pride and foolishness had separated him from his father in the far country. To be always with God does not exempt a good man from suffering but it does mean that he does not have to suffer alone. Beside him is the presence of One who cares for him and suffers with him, One to whom he can say, "I am continually with thee."

The good man is rewarded also with a sense of *God's support*, and how much better that is than being unsupported against the enemies of the body and the soul. People of British origin remember the Christmas broadcast when King George VI inspired the Commonwealth by quoting the lines, "I said to a man who stood at the gate of the year, 'Give me a light that I may walk safely into the unknown.' And he said to me, 'Go out into the darkness and put your hand into the hand of God, and it shall be to you better than a light and safer than the known way.' " Soon after that our beloved King died of cancer. He had been walking with death, and we did not know it. How helpless he was against that consuming disease which hits the righteous and the unrighteous alike! Yet how strong, because he could say to God with the Psalmist, "thou dost hold my right hand."

The good man is rewarded with a sense of *God's guidance*, and that is a blessed gift in a world where so many people are morally confused. The German philosopher, Nietzsche, was one of the few people in history who accepted moral confusion as the logical result of atheism. He knew that the denial of God meant the denial of all moral values, the denial of any real sense of direction, and he carried his "sad lantern" down all the corridors of human life and finally completed the syllogism of his logic by going mad. The godly man may have no less confusion around him for being godly but at least he himself is not confused. He knows the right way to walk. He can say his prayers and feel directed in his decisions by the indwelling Spirit of God to whom he can say, "Thou dost guide me with thy counsel."

The good man is rewarded with a *hope of glory*, and that is a blessed gift when so many people cannot see beyond the limits of life on this earth. Imagine two travellers crossing a frozen lake at night. One of them slips on the ice, falls, hurts himself and simply stays there cursing the darkness. The other slips and falls but gets up and struggles on because he can see a light on the far shore which tells him that warmth and love await him at the end of the journey. The religious man will not have an easier life for being religious; he may have a more difficult life, if religion brings him into closer touch with reality, but it will never be a life of unrelieved despair. Through all the darkness of the journey he can see the light of home and can say to God, "Afterward thou wilt receive me to glory."

One of the most inspiring sermons in the English language was preached by Arthur John Gossip in his church at Aberdeen on the Sunday following his wife's bewilderingly sudden and undreamed-of death. It has been translated into many languages, distributed in hundreds of thousands of copies and has brought comfort to countless people in sorrow and grief. Gossip called it, "When Life Tumbles In—What Then?" Speaking from the depths of personal tragedy, he said to his congregation, "Some people, when belief comes hard, fling away from the faith altogether. But in heaven's name, fling away to what? You people in the sunshine may believe the faith. We in the shadows have to believe it. We have nothing left . . ."

That's what the Psalmist decided as he grappled with his doubts in the sanctuary. It really tortured him that there seemed so little justice in God's world—why do the wicked prosper and the righteous suffer?—and he felt tempted to fling away from God altogether. In that dark hour he nearly became an atheist. Yet in that dark hour he realised that when a good man loses God he has nothing left, because God himself is the reward of a good man.

> *Whom have I in heaven but thee?*
> *And there is nothing upon earth that*
> *I desire besides thee.*
> *My flesh and my heart may fail,*
> *but God is the strength of my heart*
> *and my portion forever.*

NOTES TO PSALM 73

1. The treatment of this Psalm follows the translation in the Revised Standard Version.

Psalm 84

He Feels Envy

The subject of this chapter is envy. That's not usually a nice word because it is not usually a nice mood. In fact, it can be a very negative and destructive mood. When you envy another person you destroy your relationship with him, you wreck your own peace of mind and you set up a quarrel with God because you assume that he has dealt unfairly with you. The Bible, especially the teachings of Jesus, issues strict warnings against the corrosive power of envy in the human soul. Paul listed "envyings" as one of "the works of the flesh" (Gal 5:21 AV), and the Medieval Church included it among the Seven Deadly Sins.

Yet there is also a positive, constructive side to envy. Surely it is possible to envy people, not with resentment in your heart but with admiration, because you long to share the qualities and opportunities that make them the sort of people they are. It cannot be sinful to regard a person who stands stalwart and serene in the face of tragedy and say, "I envy his strength of character." The man who wrote the 84th Psalm displayed that right kind of envy. He envied other people their privilege of going to church. It was his reaction to their experience of God.

Listen to his passionate prayer: *"How amiable are thy taber-nacles* (How lovely are thy dwellings), *O Lord of hosts! My soul longeth, yea, even fainteth for the courts of the Lord: my heart and my flesh crieth out for the living God."* That man wanted to go to church as desperately as a person dying of thirst wants a drink of water. We don't know who he was, though we do know that he lived in the land of the Bible several centuries before Christ. Some commentators believe that he must have been a devout Jew who went up to one of the great temple feasts every year but for some reason couldn't make it this year and felt deprived. Perhaps he looked at the sun high in the sky and thought of the fortunate people worshipping God at that very moment in the temple courts: *"Blessed are they that dwell in thy house: they will be still praising thee."*

It is a rare person in the western world today who can identify himself with the writer of the 84th Psalm. We are more like the temple worshippers whom the Psalmist envied. We can go to church and worship God almost any time and anywhere we wish. In his devotional classic, *The Imitation of Christ*, Thomas à Kempis imagines the envy of Christians prevented from receiving the Lord's Supper. He writes, "For if this most holy sacrament were to be celebrated in one place only and consecrated by only one priest in the world; with how great desire dost thou think men would be affected to that place, and toward such a priest of God, that they might be witnesses of the celebration of these divine mysteries?" He goes on to say, "But now many are made priests, and in many places Christ is offered." In that privilege we are the people whom the Psalmist envies. Why? What do we have that he missed? What is or should be our experience of God in the place of worship?

To begin with, he envies us *our security in God*. That comes across in his poetic reference to God's lesser creatures whose wings give them unlimited access to the temple courts: *"Yea, the sparrow hath found an house, and the swallow a nest for herself, where she may lay her young, even thine altars, O Lord of hosts, my King, and my God."* Not that the Psalmist envied the birds. He envied a particular class of people who lived in the temple and made it their permanent home, the priests and choristers ever singing the praises of God. How privileged they were and still are!

There was a minister who said that he could never accept his annual stipend without feeling a twinge of guilt. To him it seemed like paying an athlete for playing his favourite sport or giving a salary to a mother for taking care of her children. Why should he be paid for doing the one thing in life that he most wanted to do? He had entered the ministry because he loved the church and its worship and wanted to be a part of it all the time.

He felt supremely privileged in his work. The church was his
home.

The church is home to any person who has grown up in it and
loves it. The church was home to Jesus from the very beginning
of his life. At the age of twelve he went with his parents on a
pilgrimage to the temple in Jerusalem. Along the road they
would join other pilgrims until the company grew very large as
it approached the Holy City. In the evening around the camp-
fires they would sing the Pilgrimage Psalms. Jesus would join
other children of his own age. On the return journey Mary and
Joseph discovered that Jesus was not with the other children or
anywhere in the company, so they rushed back to Jerusalem to
look for him. After searching for three days they found him in
the temple engaged in mature discussion with the Doctors of
Divinity. To their parental rebuke the boy Jesus replied almost
with surprise, "How is it that you sought me? Did you not know
that I must be in my Father's house?" (Luke 2:49 RSV)

That's what made the church home to Jesus; it was his
Father's house, the place of God's presence. "How amiable are
thy tabernacles—how lovely are *thy* dwellings—O Lord of
hosts!" Of course, God dwells everywhere, his presence fills the
universe, contains the universe. Astronauts, 250,000 miles
away from any church, have felt close to God, as one of them
did when he received Holy Communion on the surface of the
moon. Yet God's presence fills the church in such a special way
that it gives the church an atmosphere of home and gives the
worshipper a sense of security. Home should always be a secure
place, especially for a child. Out in the world he may feel lonely,
unwanted, rejected, but the all-pervading fact about his home
is the fact that his parents are present and they love him.
Therefore, he feels secure.

The all-pervading fact about the church is that God is present and he loves us. God loves us no matter where we are, but in
the church we are reminded of his love in a dramatic way. The
bread and wine in the Holy Communion are signs and pledges
of God's loving presence. They tell us that God loves us "so
much that he gave his only Son, that everyone who has faith in
him may not die but have eternal life". (John 3:16 NEB) That
makes us feel secure. In a tense, turbulent, rapidly-changing
world it gives us one eternal, unchanging, dependable reality to

which we can cling. That reality is the love of God revealed in
Jesus Christ. In the church we know ourselves embraced by
that love, accepted by it, secured by it; and in that assurance we
are to be envied.

The Psalmist envied the temple worshippers *their strength in
God*. That comes across from those verses where he says to God
in prayer, *"Blessed is the man whose strength is in thee; in whose heart
are the ways of them. Who passing through the valley of Baca make it a
well; the rain also filleth the pools. They go from strength to strength,
every one of them in Zion appeareth before God."*

It has been suggested that the Psalmist had in mind a second
group of people who were related to the temple in a different
way. He was thinking of the pilgrims travelling on foot from all
parts of the country and converging on the Holy City. For those
who came from a distance it would be a difficult and tiring
journey, perhaps even dangerous if they had to cross waterless
deserts and mountains that were infested by robbers and wild
animals. Yet each day, as they drew closer to the temple, their
spirits would rise with happy anticipation; and instead of getting weaker with the journey, they would feel themselves actually growing stronger.

On the human level they simply strengthened one another,
as people do in time of need. A man told me that several years
ago he came through a severe crisis in his life. His business went
bankrupt, he lost his job and his money, he almost went to
prison for dishonesty. About that time his twelve-year-old
daughter died of a fatal illness. It nearly crushed him completely, nearly broke his marriage. He said that he came
through because he followed the advice of a friend who said to
him, "Whatever else you do, don't drop out, don't hide yourself, don't withdraw into a shell of shame and self-pity. Stay in
circulation, keep on playing golf once a week, attend your
Rotary Club, go to church, see your friends, but don't drop
out." It was dificult for a while, but he followed the advice, he
stayed in circulation; and the loyalty, the kindness and the
support of his friends astonished him. For the first time in his
life he discovered the strength of human friendship and fellowship.

Such strength came to the ancient pilgrim on his journey to

Jerusalem. He kept going because he didn't have to go alone but was part of a company that grew larger and stronger as it approached the temple courts. Such strength comes to the modern pilgrim as he joins the crowds that approach the sanctuary on a Sunday morning. Certainly his faith grows stronger; and faith has to grow stronger or it will get weaker; it never stands still. You hear it said that churches are half-empty today because people don't believe in God. It would be true to reverse the cause and effect and say that many people have lost their faith in God because they have stopped going to church. They are like live coals removed from a fireplace and left on the hearth to die. They need to be restored to the warm, strengthening company of other believers.

It was not just the company of other believers that strengthened the ancient pilgrim but the fact that he travelled in a worshipping company. Its whole attention was focussed on God, as the attention of Christians is focussed on God and specifically upon an act of God dramatised in the Lord's Supper. The Supper symbolises the strength that God supplies. On the Communion Table are bread and wine, material food and drink that we need in order to stay alive and grow strong physically. We need also the life-giving presence of Christ, which the bread and wine represent, in order to stay alive and grow strong spiritually. Christ is present everywhere, but the church's sacramental worship is the focal point of his presence. People who receive the Sacrament in faith come away with their faith made stronger, their spirits made stronger, their own strength supplied by the strength of God. Such people are to be envied.

The Psalmist envied the temple worshippers *their sufficiency in God*. That comes across from the familiar verse, *"For a day in thy courts is better than a thousand. I had rather be a doorkeeper in the house of my God, than to dwell in the tents of wickedness."*

Commentators suggest that here the Psalmist was thinking not only about the temple worshippers but about himself and his own relationship to the temple. Though he could not go to the house of God, yet he continued to look toward the house of God. Though he couldn't always be in church, yet he could always be related to the church, and in that relationship he felt

highly favoured. It has been speculated that he might have
been a soldier on guard duty in the desert who wished that he
could stand guard for one day at the gate of the temple. "For a
day in thy courts is better than a thousand." Perhaps he saw in
the distance the encampment of the enemy and murmured, "I
had rather be a doorkeeper in the house of my God than to
dwell in the tents of wickedness."

Only once have I heard a sermon on the doorkeeper text. It
was given by a distinguished guest preacher in the church
which I served for a few years in Britain. As he entered the front
door he greeted the verger and said, "I am going to talk about
you today. My text is, 'I had rather be a doorkeeper . . .'." He
didn't know that the text fitted like a glove. Most of his life the
verger had lived in one of the African countries where he had a
lovely home and a well-paying government job with 250 men
under him. He didn't like the racist regime, however, and when
he finally couldn't stand it any longer he left his work and home
and property and emigrated to England. At his age the only job
he could find in England was that of caretaker of a church, but
he and his wife were happy at it, happier than they had been for
years. Ask him if he wanted to return to his old life, and he could
have replied literally. "I had rather be a doorkeeper in the
house of my God, than to dwell in the tents of wickedness."

The Psalmist was not a doorkeeper in the house of his God.
He was miles removed from the temple courts and envious of
those who worshipped there. His words imply that in communion with God they found a sense of sufficiency that no material
benefits could provide. That is a recurring theme in the Psalms:
"Thou art my Lord; I have no good apart from thee" (16:2
RSV); "Whom have I in heaven but thee? and there is none
upon earth that I desire beside thee" (73:25 AV); "The Lord is
my shepherd; I shall not want" (23:1 AV)—all of them varia-
tions on the light-hearted song in George Gershwin's *Porgy and
Bess*, "I've got plenty of nothing . . . but I've got my Lord."
Those Hebrew poets had plenty of nothing—no money, no
property, no status, no material security—but they had their
Lord, and that was enough.

Was it enough? Does a sense of the presence of God in
worship really provide a sufficiency that no material benefits
can provide? Turn the question around and ask whether the

possession of this world's goods will do for us what experience has proved that God can do. Will material things make us content with our lot in life? Will they calm our souls under pressure and tension? Will they help us make the right decision in a world that is morally confused? Will they supply us with courage when our life is endangered even to the point of death? Will they give us a hope that reaches into eternity? Those are the things in life that add up to a sense of sufficiency; and the Psalms sing of the sufficiency of God, the God who meets us in the holy place and supplies our every need.

Such sufficiency comes to a Christian in the Sacrament of Holy Communion. The meal is not large on the Holy Table—scarcely enough to feed a flock of sparrows. The Christian knows, however, that when Jesus, the Host who presides at his table, takes a small meal into his hands, it becomes a feast for thousands. It becomes a satisfying meal, too, that meets the deepest hungers of the soul. In this meal Christ offers security, strength and sufficiency in God. He offers himself. If we receive him in faith we are of all people the most to be envied.

PSALM 90

He Feels Temporary

Reading the 90th Psalm is like stepping inside Westminster Abbey. Its phrases are so solemn and stately. Someone called it the funeral hymn of humanity, but it is not funereal in mood, because it sings of God and his everlasting concern for man. I often read the 90th Psalm before kneeling down to pray—it gets me closer to God—and I always read it at the turn of the year. Rather than expound the Psalm in this chapter I shall try to enter the author's feelings, because they are my own feelings every time I ponder his words.

He begins, *"Lord, thou hast been our dwelling place in all generations. Before the mountains were brought forth, or ever thou hadst formed the earth and the world, even from everlasting to everlasting, thou art God."* That gives me the feeling that God has been around for a long time, and the feeling comforts me.

It always comforts me to be in the presence of someone who has been around for a long time. Recently I went to visit a man on his 100th birthday. I expected to see him propped up against pillows or hobbling around with the help of a cane, but he marched into the room like a soldier. I said, "You are in remarkably good health for a man of your age." "I certainly am," he replied heartily, "especially considering I was such a delicate child." Then he told me that he had retired in 1937. I was still in school at the time; the major part of my life had not begun. He has experienced all the important things that have happened in the world during my lifetime and many important things that happened long before I was born. I could die while he is still alive—which means that he was

here long before I came and will be here after I am gone.
When I thought about those things I felt strangely secure in his
presence.

I feel the same way after reading the 90th Psalm. The man
who wrote it looked up at the mountains which to him seemed
the oldest things in the world. He didn't know their geological
age but he did know that the mountains weren't always there.
At one time the land that thrust them upwards was as flat as a
prairie or covered with water. But God was always there, God
who made the mountains, and God will be there when they are
gone.

The mind boggles when you start thinking in terms of the
geological ages. There was a lady who cried out in horror when
an astronomer told her that the world would probably come to
an end in a billion years. He tried to reassure her by saying,
"But not before a billion years." She sighed with relief and
exclaimed, "Thank goodness! I thought you said a million." A
million or a billion—the world will come to an end because it
had a beginning. Look up at the dome of a planetarium, pick
out the tiny dot of light that represents the planet earth and
remember that once there was a blank space there. Once the
whole dome was blank and it will be blank again. But God will
be there, God who created and contains the stellar universe,
God who has no beginning or ending.

The 90th Psalm gives me the feeling that God has been
around for a long time, and I begin to think differently when I
feel that way. I don't get so uptight about a lot of things that are
coming loose in the world, things that are changing and not
always for the better. When I ask myself if there is anything
stable, anything that endures, the 90th Psalm gives me the
answer. It says, "Yes, there is the unchanging God, our dwelling place in all generations, the home of man's soul. He is
stable. He endures." It comforts me to believe in him and trust
him and commit my life to him. From everlasting to everlasting
he is God.

The Psalm continues, "*Thou turnest man to destruction, and
sayest, Return ye children of men.*" That gives me the feeling that I
am going to be around for a very short time, and I react as the
Psalmist did. I look at God's permanence and realise that I am

temporary. God is eternal but I am mortal, God endures but my life comes to an end.

Every now and then something happens to remind me of the shortness of my life upon this earth. Recently I preached at the 100th Anniversary of a church which I attended as a child. I had not been there for forty-five years. During that time the major part of my life's scenario has been played, I have completed most of my career, my children are married, and I am fast approaching the status of a "senior citizen". Yet it seemed only yesterday that I was a choirboy in that church being reprimanded by the Rector for whispering during his sermon. Forty-five years! Nearly half a century! Where has it gone? No wonder the Psalmist said that to God *"a thousand years are but as yesterday when it is past"*.

That Hebrew poet had the right idea. He knew that the time between birth and death is very short—seventy years, eighty at the most (we may have added a few). To the youth it seems time enough, but the older person asks, "Where has the time of my life gone?" It seems like a watch in the night, one of the three night watches, a third of the night; that long we are awake, that long and no longer; soon those who will replace us arrive, and we are drawn into infinite sleep again. Or like a dream which, however exciting, is quickly forgotten; or like grass which grows up in the morning and is scorched at midday; or like a flood that sweeps everything before it; or like a bird that flies away and can never be captured again. The Psalmist uses all those figures of speech. He says, *"our years come to an end like a sigh."* (RSV)

No, I am not going to be around for very long, and that's another feeling that makes me look at life differently. I begin to wish that I had made better use of it. I begin to think of all the time that I have wasted and I wish I could get some of it back; in fact, I wish I could go back to the beginning and start all over again. A comic cartoon shows a six-year-old child saying, "I wish I was three again, knowing what I know now." Some of us would settle for being thirty again, knowing what we know now. One thing for certain—we should ration the time of our life more carefully. We should count the days and the years instead of squandering them as though we had forever to live. We should pray continually with the Psalmist, *"So teach us to number our days, that we may apply our hearts unto wisdom."*

But what am I thinking about? Why am I so mournful? My life isn't over yet; I still have more time left. A minister said that when he was a young man he visited an elderly lady in her hospital room. She didn't even notice him but just kept rolling over in the bed moaning, "I don't want to die. I don't want to die." He sat through half an hour of that, did a bit of silent praying, then burst out, "You're not dead yet, are you?" She sat bolt upright and answered, "No." "Well then," he said, "get on with the business of being alive." There is a popular motto which reads, *"Today is the first day of the rest of your life"* — a good motto because it reminds us that only yesterday is dead. Today we begin life all over again and we have more days ahead of us. So we can start living right now and we can start praying right now, "Teach us to number our days, that we may apply our hearts unto wisdom."

"The days of our years are threescore years and ten; and if by reason of strength they be fourscore years, yet is their strength labour and sorrow; for it is soon cut off, and we fly away." It's not so much the shortness of life that troubles me; it's that other feeling I get whenever I read the 90th Psalm, the feeling that I am not going to accomplish very much while I am here on earth. The very shortness of life makes any real fulfilment impossible, and that makes me feel very sad. The Psalmist connects my feeling with sin. He tells me that I don't just die; God consumes me, he cuts me off, and he does so because he is angry over my wrongdoing. That apparently is why I rebel against the thought of my own death and why I feel a tragic element even in the passing of old people. I don't rebel against the death of a tree or an animal. I accept that but I don't accept man's death or even face up to it because I am guilty.

A young man came to William Ewart Gladstone, when he was Prime Minister of England, and said, "Mr. Gladstone, I should appreciate your giving me a few moments in which to lay before you the plans for my future. I should like to study law." "Yes," said the great statesman, "and what will you do after that?" "Then, sir, I should like to gain entrance to the Bar of England." "Yes, young man, and what then?" "Then, sir, I hope to have a place in Parliament, in the House of Lords." "Yes, young man, what then?" "Then I hope to do great things for Britain." "Yes, young man, and what then?" "Then, sir, I hope to retire and take life easy." "Yes, young man, and what then?" "Well then, Mr. Gladstone, I suppose I will die." "Yes, young man, and what then?" The young man hesitated and said, "I never thought any further than that, sir." Gladstone looked at him sternly and steadily and said, "Young man, you are a fool. Go home and think life through."

When we do think life through, it doesn't seem an unrelieved tragedy that we have to die. Death may actually give purpose to our human existence, it may be the reason why we accomplish anything at all. If life continued forever, it's possible that we should be permanent procrastinators, postponing every action indefinitely. The only reason I get books written is that I have to meet a publisher's deadline, without which I might never finish or even get started at any of them. Life is like painting a picture. You can't take forever at it. You have a limited time in which to work. You've got a deadline and you don't know when the deadline is. That's what impels you to work hard and try to finish the picture. You know that any moment you will be called away and you may have to leave it unfinished.

Of course, an unfinished painting is not worthless or meaningless. Some of the unfinished things are among the most beautiful things in life. Like Schubert's famous Symphony they are all the more beautiful for being unfinished. That is a comforting thought, though I must admit that it doesn't always comfort me. I want to finish the painting. In fact, when I was young I planned to do half a dozen paintings. Like the young man who came to see Mr. Gladstone I wanted to do great things with my life. Now I look back and see how few of them I have accomplished and how little I have made of my life. There just hasn't been enough time. Life comes to an end too soon. Some day I shall die unfulfilled, and that gives me a feeling of quiet despair.

Then I come to the last verse of the Psalm: "*And let the beauty of the Lord our God be upon us; and establish thou the work of our hands upon us; yea, the work of our hands establish thou it.*" That gives me a different feeling. It cheers me up and changes my despair to hope. It tells me that I don't have to finish the painting. God will finish it, he will establish the work of my hands, he will bring my life to fulfilment. I have that faith and I offer that prayer after reading the 90th Psalm.

I think of what it means in terms of the upbringing of my children. Like most parents I am quite unreasonable. I want far more for my children than any human being can possibly achieve. During the years when they were under my care I tried to influence them toward what I considered to be their life's potential. Then I saw that the time of parental influence is frighteningly short. Before you know it they are asserting their own wills and being dictated to by their friends and professors and radio gurus and a host of other influences that may be hostile to parental influence. Yet the Psalmist tells me that my parental love was not wasted. God will establish it and bring it to fulfilment, if not in my lifetime, in their lifetime or even in the lifetime of their children's children.

So with my work in the Christian ministry. I have never been the sort of minister who left a congregation with the satisfied feeling that his work there was done. I have always come away with a feeling of resentment that, after working as hard as humanly possible, I still had to leave so much undone. Some day I shall retire with the same feeling of frustration. That's why it helps to read the 90th Psalm which tells me that God will bring every noble dream to fulfilment and every righteous purpose to fruition. I can hear the Psalmist saying, "So you have planted a few trees here and there. Surely you don't expect to see them growing before your very eyes. It is enough that you planted them. God will make them grow."

So with any contribution that I have made to the Kingdom of God on earth, though I am inclined to ask, What contribution? If I have made any, I can't see it. I entered the ministry because I believed that Christ was building his Kingdom through the church and I wanted to be part of that Kingdom-building. I believed that I could really change the world. That was more than thirty years ago, and I don't see many changes. Inwardly the world looks pretty much the same. Then I read the 90th Psalm, and it asks, "How do you know?" Jesus said that you can't see the Kingdom of God in its process of growth. It works secretly and silently. Only God establishes the Kingdom, and I am not God. I am called to trust God, to be faithful, to give him my obedience in the hope that he will accept it and use it.

Those are some of my feelings after reading the 90th Psalm. I have a sense of security, yet also a sense of sadness and despair; though the Psalm leaves me with a feeling of hope, and if I don't find that hope in the Old Testament I find it in the New. It begins with the birth of a Baby who grew up in spite of some vicious attempts to stop him. When he came to manhood he showed us the most significant life ever lived on this earth—our life in the purpose of God. It was a short life by this world's measurements—not threescore and ten years but one score and ten. God consumed it and cut it off because of sin, man's sin. But God has established that life and is bringing it to glorious fulfilment. Because of Jesus we hope that God will establish our lives.

PSALM 91

He Feels Secure

How shall we explain the box-office appeal of the many disaster films that the motion picture industry has produced in recent years? All seem to follow the same basic plot. Heedless of any warnings, life proceeds at its merry pace. Then suddenly comes the explosion, the fire, the shipwreck, the earthquake, tearing bridges and buildings and highways apart as though they were cardboard models (which they probably were in the photography), showing how fragile and vulnerable are the strongest inventions of men. Masses of people are crushed like flies, countless others are maimed, injured, bereaved and homeless. The stench of death is everywhere. When the dust settles, a few lonely survivors struggle out into the sunlight to survey the wreckage and start life all over again. Why the popularity of such films? Do we secretly enjoy a disaster as long as it is make-believe and as long as all those terrible things are happening to other people and not to us?

That is the picture in the 91st Psalm. The unknown author conjures up some of the worst disasters in his world—war, plague, famine, pestilence, the attacks of reptiles and wild beasts. He puts himself in the position of a film-viewer who sees them happening to other people but knows that they are not going to happen to him. Even when he is exposed in the flesh to those perils he comes through them unscathed, he has a charmed life, he feels a perfect sense of security. Why? The answer seems very naive. He trusts in God whom he poetically describes as his refuge, his fortress, his shield, his hovering protector. *"He that dwelleth in the secret place of the most High shall abide under the shadow of the Almighty."*

Devout believers have always found comfort in the 91st Psalm. They have read it aloud in times of stress and danger, and it has sounded like the very voice of God telling them not to be afraid. Yet we suspect that the Psalm itself belongs to the realm of make-believe and is further away from the facts of real life than are the Hollywood disaster films. At least they show the impartial nature of catastrophe. They do not suggest that the few survivors were particularly good people who said their prayers and went to church and trusted in God. On the contrary, some of the finest and most devout characters perished. The shadow of the Almighty did not protect them. No Divine Providence came to their rescue. They enjoyed no special security because of their goodness and godliness. In the Bible as a whole, especially in the teachings of Jesus, God does not promise such security.

That may be true, yet to press that point would be to miss the truth of the 91st Psalm. Whether or not religious faith actually secured him against disaster, the fact remains that the Psalmist *felt secure*. That was his reaction to God, and in that important sense the Psalm *is* true to real life. As for the picture of a godly man walking unhurt through animal traps, snake pits, bloody war and devastating disease—much of that can be seen as extravagant oriental poetry. C. S. Lewis, who was a Professor of Poetry, wrote a charming little book on the Psalms in which he says, "Most emphatically the Psalms must be read as poems; as lyrics, with all the licences and all the formalities, the hyperboles, the emotional rather than logical connections, which are proper to lyric poetry. They must be read as poems to be understood; no less than French must be read as French or English as English. Otherwise we shall miss what is in them and think we see what is not."[1] The truth of the 91st Psalm, that we must not miss, is that faith in God made the author feel secure, as it makes any person feel secure; and we have to ask—In what does his sense of security lie?

It lies in the fact that *he is not obsessed with life's disasters*. He names some of them, but they do not occupy his mind to the exclusion of all else. Many people feel insecure not because of what might happen to them but because they are obsessed with the thought of what might happen. They have over-active imaginations. They lie awake at night and picture themselves in all those terrible circumstances. Even when they have taken out every conceivable insurance policy they still project disaster films on the screen of their minds.

The Psalmist poetically describes some of our worst fears. *"Thou shalt not be afraid for the terror by night; nor for the arrow that flieth by day; Nor for the pestilence that walketh in darkness; nor for the destruction that wasteth at noonday."* That is figurative language. "The terror by night" can be seen as a figure of death; and some people, especially as they grow older, are so obsessed with that fear that they cannot think or speak about anything else. "The arrow that flieth by day" could be seen as a figure of the atomic bomb or the industrial strike or the business take-over or the threat to one's marriage—the weapons of human hostility and conflict that can keep us in constant fear. "The pestilence that walketh in darkness" is surely a figure of the hidden virus germ, the sudden heart attack, the growth of malignant cells in the body, the lurking illness that comes upon us like a thief in the night. "The destruction that wasteth at noonday" could be a figure of middle-age which for many people becomes the most critical, most exhausting, most wasteful, most destructive period in their lives. Those are real disasters, not imaginary, and the thought of them can become so obsessive that they paralyse a person and keep him in constant fear.

The author of the 91st Psalm is well aware of all the terrible things that can happen to him but he is not afraid because he is not obsessed with them. He is obsessed with God. He sees life's disasters only in terms of their relationship to God. He mentions them only to glorify God. His prayers are not a recital of his own troubles, weaknesses and fears but rather an affirmation of faith in the power and purpose of God to deliver him from his troubles, weaknesses and fears. He brings his tiny field to God's sky, his filament of wire to God's electric power, his human poverty to God's Divine abundance. That is why he feels secure.

He feels secure also because he believes that *God is beside him in life's disasters*. He can walk safely through all the perils of his pilgrimage because he has the presence and frienship of God. When this Psalm was used in the Jewish temple liturgy, the closing words were spoken by a priest as though spoken by God: *"He shall call upon me, and I will answer him: I will be with him in trouble . . ."*

It is comforting to know that God shares our trouble and answers our prayers by being with us in life's disasters, but what security does it offer? The disasters still happen, and God does not protect us against them. Of course, neither does anything else protect us. We assume that enough money in the bank will insulate us against trouble, but there are just as many rich patients as poor patients in a hospital for incurables. We discover new medicines and develop new surgical skills, yet they are defeated by the increasing number of diseases of civilisation. We invent sophisticated weapons of defence, only to read in the newspapers that our enemies have invented weapons of attack that can penetrate them. The truth is that no ingenuity, no technique, no human power can protect us against what Shakespeare called "the slings and arrows of outrageous fortune". We can only turn to God in prayer.

The scene that comes to mind took place some twenty years ago when I preached at a church where the people were passing through a period of deep anxiety. Their brilliant and beloved minister, at the very peak of his career, had been stricken by cancer of the spine. Every day the chains of that dreadful disease tightened their grip on him, though he had not yet conceded its victory. The congregation prayed for him without ceasing. In the half hour before every worship service a small group came together and fervently implored God to protect their friend against the worst that could happen to him. In spite of the fervent prayers offered on his behalf, the minister died. If prayers had not been offered on his behalf he would still have died, and can we assume that they made no difference to him? Is it not possible that they had something to do with his serenity in suffering, his courageous acceptance of death, and the hope which he shared with his family that, even if he died, God's purpose for his life would not be defeated? Whether he was secure or not, the fact remains that his own faith and the prayers of his people gave him a sense of security. Like the Psalmist, *he felt secure*.

Before ruling it out as valueless, we should understand that prayer is a means of meeting God and opening our lives to his

comforting and transforming power. The man of faith may still
suffer and die but he does not have to suffer and die alone.
Beside him is a presence. One who cares for him intimately,
enters into all the feelings of his infirmities and surrounds him
with the atmosphere of an eternal and inseparable love. That
was the experience of John G. Paton, the great missionary to
the New Hebrides. After three months on those islands he lost
his young wife and had to dig her grave with his own hands,
surrounded by savage and hostile faces. Later he said, "I
should have gone mad and died beside that lonely grave if it
had not been for Christ and the love he vouchsafed to me
there."

The author of the 91st Psalm feels secure in the faith that *no
evil will happen to him in the midst of life's disasters.* This Psalm has
the dubious distinction of being the only passage of scripture
which, to our knowledge, has been quoted by the Devil. Actually the Devil misquoted it. He urged Jesus at the outset of his
ministry to play for popularity by performing the stunt of
throwing himself down from the pinnacle of the temple, trusting God to protect him from being crushed on the stones below.
"If thou be the Son of God, cast thyself down: for it is written,
He shall give his angels charge concerning thee: and in their
hands they shall bear thee up, lest at any time thou dash thy
foot against a stone." (Matt 4:6 AV) That comes close enough
to the words of the Psalmist. (vv 11,12) Jesus retorted, "It is
written again, Thou shalt not tempt the Lord thy God." Jesus
knew that only a child of God who is living in the will of God can
expect the protection of God, and even then he has no guarantee of being shielded from all harm. He knew, moreover, that
being smashed on the rocks was not the worst thing that could
happen to him. The worst was to let his character and career be
smashed by the Devil.

Against that disaster God does guarantee his protection.
"There shall no evil befall thee," writes the Psalmist. Of all the evils
that can befall a person as a result of disaster the worst is
bitterness. The Devil really gets a stranglehold on any person
when exposure to life's perils makes him bitter; and the reason
is that bitterness becomes the breeding ground of so many other
evils. It breeds cynicism, self-pity and moral laxity; makes a

person sour and crabbed and miserable, so that he poisons the atmosphere around him. There was a period in Jewish history, following the return from exile in Babylon, when God's people became intolerant to the point of cruelty. They lost much of their early idealism and altruism. They became a tight little society, looking out for number one and caring nothing for the nations around them. The awful experience of the exile had driven iron into their souls, and they felt bitter.

That can happen to the finest person. It nearly happened to a bright, attractive, energetic girl named Joni Earekson who discovered tragically that God's angels do not bear us up in their hands, lest we dash our foot against a stone. One day in 1967 she dived into a shallow part of Cheasapeake Bay and struck her head on a rock. When they dragged her out of the water they found that she was paralysed. She had broken her neck. Joni became bitter when the doctors told her that she would never walk again and never use her hands. She lay in her stryker frame nursing a deep resentment against God who had allowed her to be changed from a happy, active teen-ager to a wretched piece of useless flesh. The knowledge that she wasn't even capable of committing suicide made her even more bitter. Gradually, through the ministry of loving friends, she realised that her bitterness was destroying her and making everybody around her miserable. She turned to God and found that she no longer demanded justice or thirsted for vengeance because of the promise of life which had been taken away from her. She began to invest what little spark of life she had. After several operations and months of intensely painful effort she was able to sit up in a wheelchair. She eventually learned to draw with a pen in her mouth. Today she shows her art across North America, she has written a book about herself, she speaks to groups and individuals about the power of God to protect her against evil. Like the Psalmist this brave quadraplegic girl really feels secure.[2]

The Psalmist feels secure in the faith that *God will deliver him from life's disasters*. He specifically expresses that faith: "*Surely he shall deliver thee from the snare of the fowler, and from the noisome pestilence.*" Twice he hears the voice of God confirming his faith: "*Because he hath set his love upon me, therefore will I deliver him . . . I will be with him in trouble; I will deliver him, and honour him."*

At this point the Psalmist might seem to be going around in circles. Does he assume that God will, in fact, immunise him against the perils of life and snatch him out of the disasters which are happening to people who have no faith? Perhaps a more accurate meaning of the word "deliverance" is suggested by a popular novel by that name which was made into an exciting disaster film also called *Deliverance*. It is the story of four business men on a weekend canoe trip down a raging river. The trip begins as a lark but turns into a nightmare as they run into unexpected dangers, finding themselves imperilled by angry physical nature and by depraved human nature. They do not escape disaster but they come through it almost miraculously. They are delivered. In that sense the faith of the 91st Psalm may be true to real life.

The whole story of God's dealing with his people in the Old Testament is a story of miraculous deliverance. The God whom the Psalmists praised and trusted was the God who delivered their fathers from slavery in Egypt, brought them across the Red Sea and led them through the perils of the wilderness to the Promised Land. He was the God who delivered a later generation from exile in Babylon and brought them back to rebuild the ruins of their shattered country. He did not protect them against disaster but he brought them through it and delivered them from it. Their one great hope which kept them alive and enabled them to endure the oppression of successive conquerers was the hope that God would send a Deliverer. At the birth of Jesus angels announced the fulfilment of that hope, "Today in the city of David a deliverer has been born to you—the Messiah, the Lord." (Luke 2:11 NEB)

Like many of the Psalms this one brings us into the presence of Christ and foretells the experience of Christ. Though he prayed that God would not let it happen to him, he had to suffer the worst of all disasters, death on a Cross. Yet God delivered him from the Cross and brought him through to the triumph of Resurrection. The God of the Psalmist is the God who raised Jesus Christ from the dead. To trust that God is to feel secure in his almighty power, in his loving friendship, his protection against evil and his power to bring us through the worst disas-

ters that can happen to us. It is the security that Paul felt when
he looked at all the terrible things which had happened to him
and said, "For I reckon that the sufferings of this present time
are not worthy to be compared with the glory which shall be
revealed in us." (Rom 8:18 AV)

NOTES TO PSALM 91

1. C. S. Lewis, *Reflections on the Psalms*, Collins Fontana Books, 1976, p. 10.
2. Joni Earekson, *Joni* (World Wide Publications, Minneapolis, 1976).

Psalm 100

He Feels Joyful

Convictions is the title of a book by the Archbishop of Canterbury which contains a collection of addresses and sermons given at various times during his distinguished career. In the first one, called "Retrospect and Prospect", he takes a look at the present state of the church, gives thanks for some encouraging signs of life and expresses hopes for its future. One hope is the recovery of joy. He says,

> My hope is that the Church in the next few years will recapture its joy. Should I be misunderstood if I said that in recent years we have had something of a surfeit of ecclesiastical breast beating? Of course, the Church has plenty to repent of, so let us repent, and do it thoroughly. But let us not go to the world as if we had nothing to be thankful for. God has worked gloriously through his Church again and again, and is doing so today.[1]

The Archbishop is right. A joyless church is a contradiction in terms. Of all people on earth Christians should be the most joyful, yet of all people on earth Christians are sometimes the most doleful. At least, that's what often comes across on Sunday mornings, and it not only surprises strangers but saddens them.

Such was the experience of a remarkable Christian woman, Gert Behanna, who in her later years became a popular author and lecturer. She had been a New York socialite who by middle-age had made a total wreck of her life, then found Jesus

Christ and was healed in body and soul. She wrote a magazine article saying that she had never been to church before her conversion but she went there eagerly, looking forward to meeting the lucky people who had known Jesus for years. She expected them to be ecstatic in their joy and she felt sure they would warm her heart with enthusiasm and love. Instead, she was chilled by their gloom and sheer unfriendliness. She thought that it might be an isolated experience, so she made the rounds of several churches. In every congregation she found the same long-faced, listless people and felt bewildered. She asked, "How could they come into God's presence Sunday after Sunday without breathing in the joy that danced in the very air?"[2]

How indeed? Especially when they take upon their lips the most joyous words ever written: "*Make a joyful noise unto the Lord, all ye lands. Serve the Lord with gladness; come before his presence with singing . . .*" Such is the 100th Psalm, commonly called the Jubilate. In its Old Testament form or its metrical version composed by William Kethe, the sixteenth-century Scotsman and friend of John Knox, it is the Psalm most frequently used in synagogue services and in Christian worship throughout the world. There is scarcely a week, scarcely a day when God is not praised with the familiar words, "Make a joyful noise unto the Lord, all ye lands . . ." or "All people that on earth do dwell, Sing to the Lord with cheerful voice . . ." A cheerful voice! Why not a cheerful heart? The Psalmist's words of joy! Why not his spirit of joy?

The answer is that we have to share the secret of his joy. The Psalm itself makes clear that it was not a contrived mood, not a bubbling emotion and frothy sentiment that he manufactured in the presence of God. The joy of the author of the 100th Psalm grew out of his creed. Actually it was his response to his own deep convictions about God. He tells what those convictions are, he celebrates them; and if we could celebrate them we might possess the secret of his joy.

First, he celebrates the conviction that there is one God and that he has created us. "*Know ye that the Lord he is God: it is he that hath made us, and not we ourselves.*"

Originally the Psalm was a hymn sung by the Israelites during one of the great religious festivals when they gave thanks to God for his many mercies. It consists of two parts—the call to worship and the grounds for the call. The first part was sung by a choral group at the head of a procession moving up to the temple gates; the second was a response by another choir inside the temple, bidding the worshippers enter the temple courts. We came close to capturing that scene at the Coronation of Queen Elizabeth II and again at her Silver Jubilee Service in St. Paul's Cathedral when choir and congregation alternated the verses of the familiar paraphrase, "All people that on earth do dwell . . ." Then, as in ancient Israel, the Jubilate was a hymn of unrestrained gladness and joy, a summons to the whole earth to join in the joyous worship of God.

Its joy resides in the very fact that it *is* a hymn of worship, focussing upon the glory and goodness of God in his sanctuary. It does not begin with the human predicament, as many of the more private Psalms do. Some of them express man's sorrow over his own sin, others a mood of shame as they contrast human impurity against Divine holiness. Others protest bitterly against the injustices of life and plead with God to destroy their enemies. In private prayer the Psalmists brought all their guilts and doubts and fears and questions out into the open. In the place of worship, however, they concentrated not on the need of man but on the greatness of God. The temple was a place for affirmation: "Know ye that the Lord he is God; it is he that hath made us, and not we ourselves."

"The *Lord* he is *God*." The word "God" is a singular word. There might be many Lords in the ancient world but there could be only one God, and the Lord of Israel had proved himself to be God by doing for his people what only God could do. He had redeemed them from bondage in Egypt, entered into a covenant with them at Mount Sinai, led them across the wilderness and settled them in the promised land. In a word, he made them—not only as individuals but as a nation, a religious community. Christians celebrate the same truth when they recall the mighty acts of God in Christ that created and constituted them into a church: ". . . it is he that hath made us, and not we ourselves".

That is a joyous affirmation to make Sunday after Sunday. In our idiom it is a way of saying that man is not God. He can do many things but he cannot do all things and he doesn't have to do all things. The popular belief that speaks of "man come of age" and recognises no God but "the ground and depth of our being" pays a compliment to man but also robs him of his joy. Instead of exhilarating and challenging him, it plunges him into the posture of breast-beating that the Archbishop of Canterbury deplored. Its call to worship is what David Read offered as "a revised substandard version" of Psalm 100: "Make a dismal noise unto the Lord, all ye lands. Serve the Lord with sadness: come before his presence with groaning. Know ye that the Lord is a dead image: it is we that have made him and not he himself."[3] Modern theology has a sense of the tragic dimension of life but so little sense of life's joy.

Contrast the theology of Karl Barth whose great message was, Let God be God and let man be man instead of trying to be as God. There was joy in Barth's theology, a merriness of spirit that reflected the spirit of the man himself. Barth bubbled with joy. On the one occasion when I met him at his home in Basle he laughed continually and infected me with his childlike delight. He had a sparkling sense of humour that enlivened his conversation and lectures and writings. One of his books he dedicated to himself and followed the inscription with a quotation from Martin Luther to the effect that if he became conceited in his achievements he need only feel his ears and he would discover that he had grown "a splendid pair of big, long, shaggy asses' ears". Such was the humility of the man and his childlike joy. Like the Psalmist, Barth did not manufacture his joy. It derived from his creed, the conviction that there is a God above and beyond us, a God who created and governs and controls. "Know ye that the Lord he is God; it is he that hath made us, and not we ourselves." That is the secret of joy.

In the sanctuary before God the Psalmist celebrates another conviction. He affirms that God not only created us but adopted us and claimed us as his own. ". . . *we are his people, and the sheep of his pasture.*"

That old figure of speech may not mean much to modern city-dwellers but it meant a great deal to people in rural Palestine where the shepherd tending his flock is still a familiar sight. It occurs continually in the Old and New Testaments, most memorably in the 23rd Psalm, "The Lord is my shepherd; I shall not want". The author, himself a shepherd, thinks of how he cares for his flock, and the conviction floods his mind that God cares for his people in exactly the same way. As the shepherd is responsible for each animal in his charge, so God cares for every person as though he cared for that person alone. As the shepherd cares actively for the sheep, so God does not watch over us passively but involves himself in our lives to lead and comfort and rescue and restore. As the shepherd is concerned for the total welfare of his flock, so God is concerned for all our physical, mental, emotional, moral and spiritual needs.

There is a difference between the two Psalms. The earlier author, who presumably was King David, thought about God's care for persons, while the later Psalmist saw the nation Israel as God's special flock. ". . . *we* are his people, and the sheep of his pasture." That was no exclusive relationship. To be sure, the early Hebrews thought of the Lord as a tribal deity whose concern was limited to the people in his own territory, but the events of their history took them beyond that narrow nationalism and inspired them with faith in the redemption of all mankind. The author of the 100th Psalm saw God as the Lord of the whole earth. That's why he summoned all lands to join him in his joyous paean of praise. All are "his people and the sheep of his pasture".

Christians celebrate that truth in their worship when they sing the Jubilate after the reading of the Gospel. The Gospel proclaims the good news that the God who created us also adopted us. He came where we are and claimed us as his own. He sent the Good Shepherd to call us by name and lead us through the wilderness and lay down his life for the sheep. The philosophers were wrong when they painted a picture of God as a distant Deity sitting on a sunny mountain top, indifferent to the struggles and sufferings of his human creatures. God is not neutral. He is on our side. He has thrown in his lot with us, made our life his life, our peril his peril, our suffering his suffering. We are not orphans in an uncaring universe. We are the children of a heavenly Father who loves us and cares for us as a shepherd cares for his sheep.

When people celebrate that truth, their sorrow is turned into joy; and that is one of the recurring miracles of the religious life. Jesus promised it to his disciples when he said in the upper room, "So you have sorrow now, but I will see you again, and your hearts will rejoice and no one will take your joy from you." (John 16:22 RSV) Sorrow-into-joy is the miracle that should happen whenever Christians stand in the presence of Christ and especially when they celebrate his love in the Holy Sacrament. Sorrow-into-joy is a very human experience. It happens to a child who has been fighting with other children and who comes to his home with torn clothes and hurting limbs and tear-stained face and throws himself into the comforting arms of a parent. There he sobs out his sorrow, there he draws a sympathy, a strength and a security that turn his sorrow into joy. It is a picture of man before God. It is the secret of joy.

The Psalmist celebrates a third conviction. He affirms that God not only created and claimed us but that he has promised to stay with us forever. We may trust his goodness and love and enduring faithfulness. *"For the Lord is good; his mercy is everlasting; and his truth endureth to all generations."*

That is an amazing creed, considering the circumstances out of which it arose. The 100th Psalm was written in the period after the Jews returned to their own country from sixty years of exile in Babylon. It was a grim period. They found Jerusalem desolate and the temple a heap of ruins. They set to work to reclaim the land, restore their homes and rebuild the temple, but on every side they ran into difficulties. Even nature seemed to fight against them, sending drought and withholding the harvest. Ruthless and powerful enemies tried to cut off their building supplies and sabotage their work. God's people felt so threatened, so poverty-stricken, so overwhelmed by grief and melancholy that Nehemiah, the governor of Jerusalem, ordered them to show a more cheerful spirit, for, as he said, "the joy of the Lord is your strength." (Neh 8:10 RSV) It was then, when the prevailing mood was one of dejection and sorrow, that an unknown prophet, probably an associate of Nehemiah, issued this summons to jubilant religion, "Make a joyful noise unto the Lord . . ."

To some people that must have sounded like a mockery. Imagine saying to the few surviving Jews in Europe after the Second World War, "Make a joyful noise unto the Lord . . ." As one writer trenchantly says, "At best God is a Jewish uncle who forgot to show up for the Bar-Mitzvah; at worst, a faithless lover who fled for his own safety when the bullies and rapists approached . . . Any traditional belief in the God of Abraham, Isaac and Jacob expired forever in the gas ovens of Europe. The failure of God to deliver six million of his Chosen People out of the hands of Hitler, Rosenberg, Goebbels, Eichmann and the rest disqualified him and his claims to a covenant relationship with the Jews. Thereafter, all that remained of a historic union between God and the Jews was memory."[4] So it might have been after the Exile and so it would have been if courageous spirits had not dared to stand in the temple courts and affirm their stubborn creed that "the Lord is good; his mercy is everlasting; and his truth endureth to all generations". That was the secret of their joy.

Belief in God's goodness and mercy and enduring truth has always been the secret of joy. So it was for the Apostle Paul who wrote a little letter to his friends at Philippi in which the words "joy" or "rejoice" occur no less than fifteen times. One verse, as the New English Bible translates it, has the delightful character of a Christmas greeting: "I wish you all joy in the Lord. I will say it again: all joy be yours." (4:4) Yet it must have been a special kind of joy that possessed Paul. It couldn't have been a temperamental joie de vivre or the buoyancy of vigorous health or worldly comfort and success. Paul had none of those things. He had a naturally serious temperament, he suffered from a chronic illness; and the table on which he wrote this joyous letter was located in "death row" in a Roman prison. So how can he be joyful and wish his readers joy? The answer is that he doesn't wish them "joy". He wishes them "joy in the Lord". That phrase "in the Lord" contains the secret of joy.

It is the secret of Jesus in the upper room where the atmosphere is anything but joyful. Within twelve hours he will be on the Cross, and nothing can save him from it. His disciples know that he must die, and their hearts break with grief. They cannot comfort him, but he comforts them. In that short space of time he bequeaths an imperishable legacy of spiritual gifts that will be theirs and ours throughout all eternity. One of them is the gift of his own joy. "These things I have spoken to you, that my joy may be in you, and that your joy may be full." (John 15:11 RSV) Imagine a man about to be executed talking of joy, happiness, gladness. Either he has gone mad or he has a secret of joy that his enemies cannot touch. Of course, Jesus did have a secret. "Believe in God," he told the disciples. Believe that there *is* a God, that he is sovereign, that he cares for us and will stay with us forever.

That was the secret of joy for one of the most beloved and popular entertainers of our time. In the middle of the summer before he died he sent a Christmas card to his friends. He knew that he was dying and would not be around to greet them at Christmas. It was a plain blue folding card. On the front was printed his name, DUKE ELLINGTON, and above and below he had written by hand, "*Merrie Christmas . . . Happy New Year . . . Love*". Inside were the following lines which he evidently composed:

> I don't light a lamp to see the Sun
> Don't need proof of GOD,
> Because I know that there ain't
> a-gonna be but ONE

> The silliest thing ever read,
> Was that somebody said,
>   "GOD is dead".
> The mere mention of the first word,
> Automatically eliminates
> The second and the third

Something 'bout believing that's greater than pleasure,
Something 'bout believing that's more than treasure,
Something 'bout believing that's beyond measure,
  GOD ALMIGHTY

NOTES TO PSALM 100

1. Donald Coggan, *Convictions* (Hodder and Stoughton, London, 1975) pp. 28–29.
2. Gert Behanna, "The Joyous Way", published in *Guideposts*, November 1968.
3. David H. C. Read, *Virginia Woolf Meets Charlie Brown* (William B. Eerdmans Publishing Co., Grand Rapids, Michigan, 1968), p. 125.
4. D. Bruce Lockerbie, "Laughter Without Joy: The Burlesque of our Secular Age", Published in *Christianity Today*, 7 October, 1977.

Psalm 104

He Feels Wonder

The 104th Psalm is an anthem of praise to God for his wonderful works in Creation and Providence. It celebrates the fact that the world was made by a conscious creative act of God; that the economy of nature, the inter-relatedness of animate and inanimate things, the adaptation of living creatures to their environment, did not happen by chance but represent the design of an intelligent Creator who is mindful of the needs of his creatures and watches over them and provides for them with loving care.

The Psalmist has steeped his mind in the thought of the opening chapter of Genesis. Living in a pre-scientific age, he does not know what future generations will offer as theories of the mode of creation, but of one thing he is convinced: "In the beginning God created the heavens and the earth . . ." Like all Hebrew poets he makes his conviction an act of praise: *"Bless the Lord, O my soul. O Lord my God, thou art very great; thou art clothed with honour and majesty . . . Who laid the foundations of the earth, that it should not be removed forever . . ."*

The Psalmist cannot contain his wonder as he surveys the marvellous design of God's creation. Here is the earth stocked like a giant storehouse with abundant supplies of water, vegetables and minerals. Here are the oceans teeming with fish and resources yet untapped. Even the cattle on their pastures and the birds of the air and the wild animals in the wilderness live by the generosity of their Creator. Here are the seasons of summer and winter, the sunshine and rain that make possible the regularity of seedtime and harvest. Here are the day and night ordering man's life according to a rhythm of work and rest and giving him the strength and opportunity to draw from nature's storehouse and subdue the earth to his needs. *"O Lord, how manifold are thy works! in wisdom hast thou made them all: the earth is full of thy riches."*

Someone suggested that when we finally stand before the great King upon his throne, and he asks, "What did you think of my world?" we may have to reply, "We didn't really notice it. We were too busy on the telephone." For the good of our souls we need to get off the telephone and lift our faces out of the newspaper and tear our gaze away from the television screen and take a good look at this world in which we have lived for a few years and will probably live a few years longer. We need to recapture the Psalmist's sense of wonder.

To begin with, *it will set us free from the illusion of independence.* The illusion, simply stated, is that evolutionary man has outgrown his need for God. By his increasing control of the universe he has pushed back the frontiers of mystery, eliminating all evidence of the supernatural; and he will go on doing this until no room is left in the scheme of things for religion. God will have been crowded out of the picture altogether.

In a simple, unsophisticated way the 104th Psalm punctures the illusion of independence. It implies that man can no more be independent of God than a child growing up in his father's house can be independent of his father. If that child were capable of mature reasoning he would realise that he did not create and does not sustain the home into which he was born. Its beauty, warmth, comfort and security reflect the intelligence, the resources and the love of those who did create and provide it for him. So the Psalmist sees all of nature as a reflection of the Lord of nature. He sees the world in which he lives as existing within the power and providence of an intelligent and loving Creator.

Of course, the Psalmist was a poet, and poets have often seen "earth crammed with heaven and every common bush afire with God." That does not mean that their insights are unscientific. A modern scientist, if he were a man of faith, would not argue with the 104th Psalm but would bring it up to date and employ modern thought-forms to express the wisdom and

power of God. The astronomer might tell us about the unique-
ness of the planet earth in our solar system, of how the earth is
so tilted on its axis as to revolve around its axis and so related to
the sun as to follow a steady path around the sun, providing for
alternate night and day, heat and cold, thereby making life on
its surface possible. The geologist might take us down to the
heart of the earth and bring us up step by step through the
geological ages, showing us the abundant resources of gold,
iron, coal, oil and uranium which were stored there long before
the arrival of man to provide the basic materials of our civilisation. The botanist might fascinate us with the picture of
nature's beauty in the chemistry of a wild flower, and the
physiologist might point to the intricate mechanism of the
human body. It is not surprising that some great scientists in
their study of nature, which Robert Boyle called "God's Other
Bible", have classed themselves among the ranks of devoutly
religious men. They have not nursed the illusion of independence.

The more we look at God's wonderful world, the more we
realise that we live in a vast givenness. We see a whole realm of
life that we did not create and could not create and where we
cannot claim to be independent. Someone has said that, though
Henry Ford and his family own the Ford Motor Company, yet
if Mr. Ford set out by himself to build one Ford car he would
soon discover his dependence on natural resources all over the
earth and within the earth which he did not create and does not
have the power to create. That is true of man himself as he flies
to the moon or splits the atom or bakes bread or plucks flowers
in his garden. Man discovers truth but he does not create it. He
works the works of God, but they are still the works of God. He
manipulates the scheme of things but he does not add to the
scheme of things. He makes new combinations and arrange-
ments but he does it within the order of God's creation and
providence.

A university president in the United States faced the
unpleasant task of disciplining a student who had wrecked
some college property. The young man jauntily produced his
cheque book and said with a bored expression, "What's the
damage? I'll pay for it." "Put it back!" thundered the President. "Tomorrow in the chapel you will make a public ack-

nowledgement of your offence or be expelled. Do you think that
with a few miserable dollars you can repay your debt to the
founders of this university, those who built this place and
endowed it at great cost? Every person here is a charity student." The 104th Psalm takes that thought a step further and
says that every person everywhere is a charity student as long
as he lives in God's wonderful world. We may wreck that world
but we did not create it and we did not endow it. We are all
debtors to God, and by no illusion of independence can we
cancel the debt.

The 104th Psalm reminds us also that *we have a stewardship*. As
we cannot claim to have created or endowed the world, neither
can we claim to own the world. We are tenants and we have to
conduct ourselves as tenants.

There is nothing unusual about the misfortune that befell a
family who went abroad for several months and leased their
house during their absence. They thought they had found
desirable tenants until they received some disturbing reports.
The new people waited for them to leave the country, then
promptly brought in two more families to share the house.
They completely neglected the property which became a dis-
grace to the neighbourhood. They threw garbage into the back
garden and left it there to rot. They broke windows, tore the bed
linen, damaged the furniture and appliances and ornaments.
They held noisy parties that lasted half the night and kept the
neighbours awake. Before long the owner had to notify his
lawyer to evict the tenants. "You would think that they owned
the place," he said afterwards.

That is the original sin of man. That's why he was evicted
from the Garden of Eden which, by all reports, was a beautiful
and idyllic place for anyone to spend the rest of his days. God
put him in there as a tenant, but he behaved as though he
owned the place. That is still the sin of man and the root of most
of his problems. Disputes over ownership of earth's resources
have caused nearly every major and minor war in history and
even now threaten to trigger off a war that will eliminate our
problems by eliminating us. The only peaceful solution is the
faith implicit in the 104th Psalm, viz., that man does not own
any of the world's resources. In the last analysis they belong

to God who created the world, sustains the world and owns the world. As a tenant in God's world man may use those resources but he has a stewardship to use them responsibly.

Ecologists confront us today with the tragic fact that man has not used his resources responsibly. He has not been a good tenant. That message comes across from James Michener's massive novel *Centennial*[1] which traces the history of the State of Colorado in the U.S.A. The story starts back in the farthest reaches of pre-history, the periods of floods and earth convulsions when God prepared the rivers, the mountains, the minerals and the soil for human habitation. It takes us through the ages of the dinosaur, the bison and the beaver. Then man enters the scene. He comes with the Indians and the first white settlers who cover the plains with the finest breeds of cattle. Man prospers at first because he respects the land and cooperates with the laws of nature. Soon, however, his cooperation turns to exploitation; and in less than two hundred years he has polluted the rivers or drained them altogether, turned the land into a dust bowl and covered it with a network of highways, so that it will no longer support livestock or even people.

That tragedy could happen on a global scale, as the economists, Barbara Ward and Kenneth Boulding, have warned us in their picture of the earth as a small spaceship cruising among the planets to an unknown destination. In that spaceship there is a limited amount of room, a limited supply of oxygen, a limited supply of food and water and a limited number of places where you can go and be quiet. The number of passengers has to be controlled, or you get the impossible situation projected for 1700 years from now when the mass of people on the earth's surface will exceed the mass of the earth itself. That spaceship has to be kept clean. If we leave garbage lying around, if we make too much noise, if we contaminate the air and food and water, we jeopardise the safety and health and the very lives of everyone aboard. There can be no inputs or outputs in the spaceship. When the resources of the atmosphere, the oceans and the soils are exhausted they are exhausted permanently. There has to be some equality of distribution. Half the passengers cannot monopolise the limited resources of food, medicines and education while the other half are literally poor, hungry, sick and ignorant. It is a wonderful spaceship, a wonderful world that God has given us as a home among the planets, but we had better take care of it, we had better recognise that we have a stewardship, or it won't be wonderful much longer.

We shall strengthen our faith if we can capture the mood of wonder in the 104th Psalm. We shall realise not only what we owe to God but what we can expect from him. We shall discover how much God loves us.

A beautiful play, based on a book by Jean Webster called *Daddy Long Legs*, tells the story of a girl in an orphanage who was befriended by an anonymous benefactor. This gentleman was so charmed by the homeless girl that across the years he maintained a silent sponsorship, caring for her at a distance, paying for her clothes, providing for her education. She never learned his identity. Even though she met him in person she did not know that he was her benefactor. Once she had seen his shadow cast from an open office door and she thought of him in terms of that shadow, a good shadow, kind and thoughtful and generous.

God is no more substantial than a shadow cast from an open office door. We have never seen God but we have seen God's world, the home that our unseen Benefactor created for us to live in. It is a wonderful world, far more rich and beautiful than anything we could ever have created for ourselves. A God who could provide us with such a world must be a good God, a kind, thoughtful, generous God. He must love us very much. We can trust him and commit our lives to him.

That is what God said to his servant Job out of the whirlwind. The first time we read in the Old Testament the story of that magnificent sufferer, who pounded on the door of heaven and dared God to come out and face him like a man, we think that God was almost cruel to hit him with a barrage of questions about the day and the night and the stars and the oceans and the wild animals. (Chaps 38–41) What possible comfort can such irrelevant questions bring to a man who has lost everything in life, including his faith in God? Yet are they so irrelevant? Ponder them carefully and you begin to realise that

God is saying to Job, "Take a good look at the world that I created for you to live in. Isn't it a wonderful world, an orderly, dependable, kindly world, and doesn't it tell you something about me? Will not the God who sets boundaries for the ocean tides also set boundaries for the destructive elements that beat on the shore of man's soul? Will not he who cares for the wild creatures also care for the noblest of his creatures? Surely the God who lavishes his love on the waste and desolate ground will not forget men and women in their wasted and desolate hearts. Trust God, Job. He loves you far more than he loves the world in which you live."

There was a political prisoner named Charney in one of Napoleon's dungeons who learned that lesson. Alone in his dark cell he became embittered, lost all faith in God and rebelliously scribbled on the wall, "All things come by chance." One morning he saw a tiny green blade of grass breaking through the hard earthen floor and struggling into the single shaft of sunlight. He was fascinated by it, the only other living thing in his cell. Each day he watered and nurtured it and encouraged its growth. The green blade became his friend and teacher and when at last it burst into a beautiful white and purple flower, Charney found himself thinking thoughts of God again. He erased the words previously scribbled and wrote in their place, "He who made all things is God". Somehow word of this incident reached the ears of the Emperor's wife. Convinced that a man who so loved a flower could not be a criminal, she persuaded Napoleon to release him. So Charney went home, taking his precious little prison flower with him and pondering in his heart the promise of Jesus who pointed to the providence of God in nature and said, "Wherefore, if God so clothe the grass of the field, which today is, and tomorrow is cast into the oven, shall he not much more clothe you, O ye of little faith?" (Matt 6:30 AV)

There is a sternness in the 104th Psalm, puncturing our illusion of independence and reminding us that this wonderful world is the Father's house and that we live here as debtors to his generosity. There is warning, too, reminding us that God has not given us the earth but entrusted it to us and that we have a stewardship to use it responsibly. There is infinite comfort as well, a strong basis for our personal faith, the visible reminder of a God who is kind and gracious and good, a God whom we can trust.

NOTES TO PSALM 104

1. Copyright © 1974 by Random House, Inc.

Psalm 127

He Feels Futile

The vacant lot next to our church in Toronto became a great, gaping hole in the ground surrounded by a high wooden fence. For a while we were afraid that the church might fall into it. Now we are afraid that the tall building which is going up in that hole will blot the church out of the landscape. It is to be an apartment hotel and will accommodate a number of families who, we hope, will be aware of the church's presence.

The men digging the foundations were aware of the church's presence. They would have been even more aware if the Rector had gone down into the hole one morning and said to the developers, architects, contractors and workmen, "You fellows are wasting your time. You should start your work every day with a prayer meeting in the church. You need the help and guidance of God. In fact, 'Unless the Lord builds the house, those who build it labour in vain'." You can imagine their rejoinder: "We respect you, Reverend Sir, but we'd respect you more if you stayed on your side of the fence. Building this apartment house is our work. The Lord has nothing to do with it."

That is the clearest possible statement of the secular point of view. It declares that God has nothing to do with engineering, labour, business, industry, politics, education, journalism, culture, morality, etc. Secularism does not deny God's existence; it simply restricts him to religion and separates him from the construction of buildings and from all other areas of life where people live and learn and work and play.

That's what concerns the writer of the 127th Psalm whom

the Rector might have quoted. He feels the futility of secularism, as indicated by the phrase *"in vain"* which he uses three times. His sense of futility is really his response to the activity of God in human experience. He can see that God is working in human affairs and he believes that only when man's efforts are in harmony with the divine purpose can true success be achieved. He marks out certain areas of life, certain common ventures and human interests where God must not be left out of account. He begins with one of our oldest concerns — the building of houses: *"Unless the Lord builds the house, those who build it labour in vain."*[1]

Be clear what the Psalmist meant when he wrote those words. He was not saying that human beings are unable to design and create a building without the help and guidance of God — though they might run into trouble without a few materials that God has created for them. The Psalmist meant that without God's help the whole project becomes an exercise in futility because, once constructed, it becomes vulnerable to disease, fire, earthquake and other mysterious forces of evil. We ask, "Isn't that true of any building?" Not in the sense that the Psalmist implied. He was thinking of sinister forces that no human creation can withstand. To be immune to them and to have any lasting result, human labour must be instructed, guided and inspired by the Spirit of God. In that sense the Lord *has* to build the house.

There is still a direct relationship between the future of a building and the spiritual state of those who designed and constructed it. That was the theme of a motion picture called *The Towering Inferno* which showed a spectacular fire in a tall apartment tower caused by the dishonesty of the subcontractors. The use of a building may affect its future. Not far from the church in Toronto is Rochdale College which began as an academic institution and became a subsidised residence for the off-beat elements in university life. They did not represent another culture, they represented a perversion of all culture. In Rochdale you could purchase any brand of narcotics, unless you were a policeman — in which case you would find that the elevators (lifts) didn't work and that someone had slashed the tyres of your car. Eventually and with some difficulty the residents were evicted, but not until they had so damaged and dirtied the building that renovation is costing taxpayers millions of dollars. That is one house that the Lord did not build.

This could be another. It was described by an intelligent, middle-aged woman who was asked in a Creative Writing Seminar to write an essay on her most precious possession. She read the piece aloud, and we were all impressed not only by its literary excellence but by its sincerity. It was about the house that she and her husband had just built, the house of their dreams which they had been planning for years. Obviously she appreciated and loved her house, almost idolised it. She gave the impression that if it were suddenly taken from her, she would be not only bereft but bereaved. She was counting on that house to provide her with renewed happiness, and that seemed a heavy burden to place on bricks and mortar. Surely happiness is decided by the more basic question, Can we make this house a home? Will it be a centre of trust and comradeship and not a mere glorified dormitory? The Psalmist answers that question. He says that without a spiritual foundation the home may eventually collapse and the whole enterprise end in futility. "Unless the Lord builds the house, those who build it labour in vain."

Soon the high-rise building next to the church will be completed. There will be families in the apartments, and we hope that some will find their way into the church. Certainly we intend to invite them. The Psalmist has a word for them, and it is a word about family life. He doesn't use the phrase, "in vain". He talks about sons being *"a heritage from the Lord"* and *"like arrows in the hand of a warrior"*—meaning that, if they are full grown by the time their father reaches old age, they can defend him against his enemies and secure justice for him if ever he is falsely accused. Some commentators suggest that here we have a combination of two Psalms with the same fundamental thought, viz., that God is working in human affairs and that only when man's efforts are in harmony with the divine purpose can true success be achieved.

That is true not only of houses but of the families who occupy them, and that is the next common venture to which the Psalmist turns his attention. He is concerned with the building not only of houses but of homes and presumably with marriage, the first act in the building of a home. Some church liturgies begin the marriage ceremony by quoting the 127th Psalm, "Unless the Lord builds the house, those who build it labour in vain." Behind it is the belief that marriage is God's gift not only for the procreation but for the happiness of his children, a happiness that they can find in no other way. Some do not find it because they try to build their own marriages. They leave God out. They enter a civil contract, not a sacred covenant, and eventually, at least in North America, join the 50 percent of all married couples who find their way to marriage clinics and divorce courts.

Beyond any doubt the whole structure of marriage today is swaying like a tall tower in a hurricane. Some people predict that it will collapse, as it is collapsing in the experience of an increasing number of couples. The answer, however, is not more marriage clinics and easier divorce laws but a concerted war on secularism, the great and pervasive enemy of our times, secularism in our own hearts and everywhere in modern society.

In Ibsen's play, *The Master Builder*, Halvard Solness declares that since he lost his children in a fire he has no heart for building church towers—only homes for human beings. "But," says a girl reflectively, "couldn't you build a little bit of a church tower over those homes as well?" That is the answer—for Solness himself and for the families who will live next door to the church. They will strengthen their family life and come through their crises by being related to the church, bringing their children to baptism and Sunday School and themselves to public worship, building not only a church tower over their homes but a spiritual foundation beneath them that no hurricane, no winds of moral and social change can ever shake.

In the recent biography of Karl Barth by Eberhard Busch there is a fine photograph that illustrates the Psalmist's word about children defending their father against his enemies.[2] It shows the great theologian climbing a mountain in Switzerland, flanked by his two sons, Markus and Christoph. The photo was taken in 1941 just after their younger brother, Matthias, had died as the result of a climbing accident; and now they were upholding their father in his hour of great grief, defending him against the enemies of his soul. Barth was proud of his sons of whom he said, "My grown-up sons are my best comrades—which is not a gift bestowed on every father." When both became teachers of theology, Markus in the United States and Christoph in Indonesia, Barth in Europe comforted himself with the thought "that the sun now constantly finds at least one of our family awake and at work in the service of the most beautiful of all sciences". Such is the stability of a family whose structure of life has been built by the Lord.

Down the street from the church and the new apartment is a police station, a friendly-looking building that should give us a sense of security. The sight of uniformed men and women setting out on foot and in patrol cars at all hours of the day and night is most reassuring. We can sleep peacefully in our beds knowing that they watch over us like guardian angels. The Psalmist has a word for them too, and it is a cautionary word as he turns to another important venture of our common life—the defence and protection of our communities: *"Unless the Lord watches over the city, the watchman stays awake in vain."* Again he is saying that God is working in human affairs and that only when man's efforts are in harmony with the divine purpose can true success be achieved.

In some situations the watchmen by themselves are not enough. They were not enough in New York on July 13, 1977 when a power failure blacked out the city for twenty-four hours and let loose a tidal wave of vandalism and looting. Some 1400 stores were robbed; 418 police officers were injured, 18 seriously; 3600 persons were later arrested, and thousands escaped arrest. More serious was the degree of public sympathy for the looters, the assumption that they were acting within their rights and taking what society owed them, and the indignation toward the police for treating them so brutally. Behind that sympathy is a frightening attitude which repudiates any kind of authority and regards the policeman not as a defender and protector but as a potential enemy.

The Psalmist sees that kind of moral anarchy as a symptom of the secular society. He sees it precisely as what happens when people leave God out of account. His thought is taken up by the eighteenth century English poet, Alexander Pope:

Religion, blushing, veils her sacred fires,
And unawares Morality expires.
Nor public flame nor private dares to shine;
Nor human spark is left, nor glimpse divine!
Lo! thy dread empire Chaos! is restor'd,
Light dies before thy uncreating word:
Thy hand, great Anarch! lets the curtain fall,
And universal darkness buries all.

In that view public safety is not only a military problem but a moral and spiritual problem. It goes far beyond the legal and penal institutions of man and includes the whole of man—his commonsense, his native decency, his culture and his religion—everything that lifts him above the animals.

In 1953 a distinguished Methodist minister in England, W. E. Sangster, emphasised that truth in a famous sermon that made newspaper headlines all over the country. He asked, "What Would a Religious Revival Do for Britain?" and he gave ten assurances: "It would pay old debts: it would reduce sexual immorality; it would disinfect the theatre; it would cut the divorce rate; it would reduce juvenile crime; it would lessen the prison population; it would improve the quality and increase the output of work; it would restore to the nation a high sense of destiny; it would make us invincible in the war of ideas; it would give happiness and peace to all the people." He was saying, in effect, that a revival of religion leads inevitably to a reformation of manners and that in the defence of society the church is just as important as the police station. Not that policemen will ever become unnecessary in this imperfect world, but "Unless the Lord watches over the city, the watchman stays awake in vain."

Surrounding the church, the police station and the new apartment are a number of office buildings that swallow their workers every morning and disgorge them every evening. The Psalmist has a word for them as he turns to another venture of our common life, the performance of daily work, and again it is a restraining word: "*It is in vain that you rise up early, to go late to rest, eating the bread of anxious toil; for he gives to his beloved in sleep.*"

Some segments in our society find that advice irrelevant.

They have never toiled anxiously and never will. They don't know what their place of work looks like early in the morning or late at night. Stress will not kill them, though they might die of moving so slowly that their blood has no chance to circulate. To them the ideal situation would be one in which they did not have to work at all.

At the other extreme are those who not only work hard but make a fetish of overwork. They may even be workaholics, compulsive workers addicted to work as a compulsive drinker is addicted to alcohol. They arrive at the office before everyone else arrives, they remain after the others have left, and when they finally go home they take work with them in a briefcase. They toil anxiously, which means that they worry about their work, they don't enjoy it or feel secure in it, they never relax. All the time they are tired and tense. Yet they are not always the great producers, they don't really accomplish more than others accomplish.

That's no mystery to the Psalmist. He says, "It is in vain that you rise up early, to go late to rest, eating the bread of anxious toil; for he gives to his beloved in sleep." Again he is saying that God is working in human affairs and that only when our efforts are in harmony with the divine purpose can true success be achieved. He even suggests that we may achieve that harmony by allowing ourselves a good night's sleep. The Authorised Version translates him here, "For so he giveth his beloved sleep"; and there is a sense in which God does give sleep, the sleep of a good conscience, of contentment, of freedom from anxiety, a sleep more dreamless and peaceful than that induced by drugs. Sleep is one of God's most precious gifts for the renewal of our bodies and souls.

The change in the Revised Standard Version is slight but significant: not "he giveth his beloved sleep" but "he gives to his beloved in sleep". The promise is that while we rest God works on our behalf. God gets through to us and deals with us, giving us even in our sleep the spiritual resources to cope with the problems we have to face next day. That thought was captured by a Frenchman, Charles Péguy, who wrote a beautiful poem entitled, "God Speaks", in which he imagines God telling us that sleep is the most beautiful thing he has created, the secret of youth and the source of renewed strength. He imagines God chiding us for refusing to entrust our business to him, even for the space of one night; as though he who governs the universe were incapable of handling the affairs of men. He imagines God calming our troubled spirits and telling us to dry our anxious tears. *"Because between now and tomorrow, maybe I, God, will have passed by your way."*

There is an alternative to the futility of secularism. It lies in the simple confidence of a Hebrew poet that God is involved in human affairs and that our common ventures will succeed only when we bring our efforts into harmony with the divine purpose. If we recovered that confidence and took it seriously into the building of our homes and families, into the defence of our community and the performance of our daily work — we should surely discover the rich, purposeful, productive quality of life for which God in his love has created us.

NOTES TO PSALM 127

1. The treatment of this Psalm follows the translation in the Revised Standard Version.
2. Published in 1976 by the S. C. M. Press, London; and Fortress Press, Philadelphia.

Psalm 130

He Feels Guilty

"Out of the depths have I cried unto thee, O Lord . . ." The person who wrote those words has plenty of company. He was in the depths, and the depths of life are a well-populated place. Most people have been there at one time or another, and the chances are that they will be there again. Crushing disappointment can plunge a person into the depths. So can tragic bereavement or physical pain. In the case of the Psalmist it was the shame of moral failure, the burden of unforgiven sin. He cried out to God from the depths of guilt.

Guilt is one of the prevailing moods in the Old Testament Psalter. There are other moods too. The Psalmists can be happy, grateful, angry, blood-thirsty and self-righteous. Next to praising God, however, their most frequent response to God is the confession of sin, the mood of penitence. Seven Psalms are specifically known as the Penitential Psalms (6, 32, 38, 51, 102, 130, 143). The church makes particular use of them during the season of Lent, but they are not popular, because guilt is not a popular emotion. Secular society regards it as negative and unhealthy. It sees the depths of guilt as a morbid state of mind which a person should escape as quickly as possible or, better still, which he should avoid in the first place. At the turn of the year a typical newspaper editorial poked fun at the old-fashioned custom of making New Year's resolutions, saying that we shall only break them anyway and feel guilty about it, and who wants to feel guilty?[1]

Other people have a more positive view of guilt. Lord Devlin, the British jurist, said in a public lecture (Nov. 9, 1964), "If

with the wave of a psychoanalytical wand you could abolish
tomorrow the sense of guilt in the human mind, it would cause
an instantaneous collapse of law and order." He might have
added that it would also cause a collapse of personal character.
Guilt serves a useful purpose not only in society but in the life of
the individual. It acts like a red signal light in his conscience
warning him against behaviour that might be hurtful to himself
and others; or like a physical pain that hits a middle-aged man
after he has jogged up a hill, warning him that if he wants to
stay alive and well he ought to go more easily in the future. A
person needn't be ashamed of guilt any more than he needs to
be ashamed of a toothache. On the contrary, it is a sign that his
conscience is morally alive.

The writer of the 130th Psalm had a positive view of guilt.
Too often he has been depicted as an utterly miserable person.
Perhaps he did feel miserable, and perhaps "the depths" from
which he cried indicate that he was physically ill and sinking
into the deep waters of death. Martin Luther, whose acute
sense of guilt made him physically ill, picked out the 130th as
his favourite among the Psalms. He recognised in the author a
kindred spirit. Both felt miserable, yet in each case it was a
positive misery. In the long run their sense of guilt contributed
more to their health than to their sickness.

Guilt turned the Psalmist to God; and whatever does that
can't be all bad. Anything in life that turns a person to God can
be called a means of grace. It may be an unpleasant experience
that we have tried to avoid but if it brings God into the picture it
ultimately works for the healing of our bodies and souls.

Many people like the Psalmist have been driven to God by
their sense of guilt. *"Out of the depths have I cried unto thee, O Lord.
Lord, hear my voice: let thine ears be attentive to the voice of my supplica-
tions."* It might be argued that if he had not turned to God in the
first place he would never have sunk into the depths of guilt.
Some psychiatrists might say to him, "Your trouble is that you
are too religious. Your belief in God gives you an exaggerated
sense of sin and makes you feel guilty. You should stop going to
church."

Of course, that's a simplistic solution—like curing a
headache by cutting off the head. It assumes that unreligious

people can do what they like and never feel guilty, which is simply not true. In the context of faith the sense of guilt becomes a sense of sin against God, but guilt itself is a moral fact that we cannot argue away and still live in a world of moral realities. The truth is that any person with any conscience at all will be more troubled about the wrong he has done and the good he has failed to do than about anything else in the world. In fact, his guilt, unless he deals with it, may make him quite wretched and may lie beneath the surface of his mind like a splinter beneath the surface of the skin.

How does a person deal with the sense of guilt? The answer is that he cannot deal with it himself. He cannot forgive his own moral failures any more than a doctor can remove his own appendix. The forgiveness, the healing, the cure must come from beyond himself. In Dostoyevsky's novel, *Crime and Punishment*, the murderer confesses his crime to a prostitute and asks her to forgive him, not because her forgiveness means anything but because he knows that he cannot forgive himself. It is at that point that many a person turns to God, perhaps for the first time in his life, certainly with a sense of dependence and desperation that he has never known before.

One of the most celebrated examples in our time is Charles Colson, the United States Government lawyer, who was arrested and sentenced for his complicity in the Watergate scandal. He went through a religious experience which he describes in his book, *Born Again*.[2] At the heart of it was a crisis of guilt which some of the other conspirators, to their own loss, did not experience. They protested their innocence and insisted that they were unjustly accused. Colson, however, from the depths of guilt turned to God, as the Psalmist did, and guilt became for him a part of the most healing experience he had ever known.

In a positive sense the Psalmist's guilt forced him to face his own frailty. Actually he pleaded the human frailty of all people: "*If thou, Lord, shouldest mark iniquities, O Lord, who shall stand?*"

He was not rationalising, not excusing himself, not saying, "I'm no saint but I am no worse than anybody else. We are all in this together." Two truths stand out in his declaration: first, an acknowledgement of the fact of sin, an admission that every man by his very nature is a sinner. The author of the First Epistle of John states the truth in even stronger language. When a class of thinkers, calling themselves Gnostics, arose in the early church and denied among other things the reality of sin, John called them liars. "If we say we have no sin, we deceive ourselves, and the truth is not in us." (I John 1:8 RSV)

So declares Dr. Karl Menninger, one of the leading psychiatrists in North America, the co-founder and director of the famous clinic in Topeka, Kansas, that bears his name. Recently he wrote a book with the provocative title, *Whatever Became of Sin?*[3] He is concerned that the word "sin", which was once a proud word, a strong, ominous and serious word, seems to have disappeared even from the Christian vocabulary, the word as well as the idea. He asks, "Why? Doesn't anyone sin any more? Doesn't anyone believe in sin?" Unlike some members of his profession, Dr. Menninger has a positive view of sin. He considers it a fact of life and the admission of that fact as essential to the health and stability of human character and society. He says, "I believe that there is 'sin' which is experienced in ways which cannot be subsumed under verbal artifacts such as 'crime', 'disease', 'delinquency', 'deviancy'. There *is* immorality, there *is* unethical behaviour, there *is* wrongdoing. And there *is* usefulness in retaining the concept, and indeed the word SIN."

The second truth that stands out in the Psalmist's declaration of his own frailty is that no person can justify himself before God. "If thou, Lord, shouldest mark iniquities, O Lord, who shall stand?" That was Martin Luther's dilemma. As a devout monk of the Church of Rome he desperately wanted to justify himself, to be righteous, i.e. to be in the right before God, and he ran the whole gamut of the Roman Catholic penitential system in order to make himself right. Instead, he only made himself ill. In the end Luther realised that God had to justify him, God must forgive him. The admission of his own frailty was the turning point for Luther and for the Psalmist, and it can be the turning point for us.

Another positive effect of the Psalmist's guilt is that it compelled him to examine his basic beliefs. Having admitted that God must forgive his sins, he cried out in faith, *"But there is forgiveness with thee, that thou mayest be feared.*" He added, ". . .*with the Lord there is mercy, and with him is plenteous redemption.*"

That is an impersonal statement the way it stands. It belongs to the sphere of academic theology or perhaps in the realm of liturgy—like reciting the Apostles' Creed, "I believe in the forgiveness of sins". Yet that is not a bad place to begin when you are in the depths of guilt and you want God to get you out. At the very least you need to know what you believe about God and what you can expect of him. Is he a pardoning God? Does he, in fact, forgive sins?

There are two popular answers to that question, both of them wrong. The first was stated by the Frenchman, Voltaire, who wrote, "Of course God forgives sins. That is his business." Many people, even religious people, speak with the same impious nonchalance. Somewhere they picked up the strange idea that God treats our sins less seriously than we treat them. They are so sure of God's moral indifference that they don't even bother to ask his forgiveness; they simply take it for granted, as did one woman who told a pastoral counsellor that she had committed adultery with several men. She felt worried that her friends would find out and disapprove but not worried that she had sinned against God. "God will forgive me," she said confidently.

The other answer was stated by Aldous Huxley who said, "There is no such thing as forgiveness," and by George Bernard Shaw who said, "Forgiveness is the beggar's refuge. We must pay our debts." That implies that God keeps score of our sins and that we must pay a penalty; otherwise there would be no justice, and the world would be a terrifying place in which to live. Can we assume that the laws of God are less sacred than the laws of society, that we can play fast and loose with them and get away scot free? Is God less responsible than a good government, less just than a human magistrate, less protective than a city policeman? If so, God has set us in a jungle, not an ordered universe. How could we respect such a God?

What, then, is the right answer, and was the Psalmist right when he said to God, "But there is forgiveness with thee, that thou mayest be feared"? What does the Bible mean by forgiveness? Surely it means more than the impersonal pardon pronounced by a judge who says, "Case dismissed" and goes home to his waiting dinner. Forgiveness is not a legal but a personal transaction, the most difficult and costly of all personal transactions, as anybody knows if he has tried to forgive or has been forgiven. There is pain and sorrow and anguish in forgiveness. It involves nothing less than a complete sacrifice of pride, going to the person who has hurt you, sharing his shame, bearing the burden of his guilt and refusing to let your friendship with him be broken. It means accepting that person, loving him and suffering with him in spite of what he has done to you. Can we be sure and how do we know that God does that for us? To say with the Psalmist, "But there is forgiveness with thee", compels us to examine our basic beliefs.

The most positive result of the Psalmist's guilt is that it put him in a mood to receive God's forgiveness, a mood of waiting and hope and expectation. *"I wait for the Lord, my soul doth wait, and in his word do I hope. My soul waiteth for the Lord more than they that watch for the morning . . ."* The picture is that of watchmen on guard at the walls of the city, looking impatiently for the first signs of dawn, knowing that, though it comes slowly, it will surely come. The Psalmist sees himself as a watchman who believes that God's forgiveness will come and who waits, perhaps impatiently, for God actually to forgive him.

A person has to make that move from theology to experience if he hopes to rise out of the depths of guilt. So it happened to Martin Luther. "Oh, my sin, my sin!" he sobbed in anguish. One day an old monk came to his cell and tried to comfort him. He told the tortured and sorrowing Luther to repeat over and over again the article of the Apostles' Creed, "I believe in the forgiveness of sins". Luther did so and found some solace in the mere repetition of the words. "Ah", said the old monk, "you must believe not only in the forgiveness of David's sin and Peter's sin. It is God's command that we believe that our sins are forgiven us. The testimony of the Holy Ghost in thy heart is this, 'Thy sins are forgiven thee'."

It is not generally known that the 130th Psalm influenced John Wesley's religious experience. Most people know that it happened one evening at a little Moravian chapel in London while he listened to a reading of Luther's Preface to Paul's Roman Epistle and felt his heart strangely warmed. When we read in Wesley's Journal the account of that day, May 24, 1738, we discover that he earlier worshipped at St. Paul's Cathedral where the anthem was, "Out of the deep have I called unto thee, O Lord". To Wesley that was a picture of his own soul. He had been in the depths for a long time. Like the Psalmist he believed that there is forgiveness with God and like the Psalmist he waited desperately for God to forgive him. That happened a few hours later when he said, "I felt that God had forgiven my sins, even mine . . ."

It is inevitable that forgiveness should be at the heart of the Christian experience, because forgiveness is at the heart of the Christian Gospel. The central event in the Gospel is a Man dying on a Cross to make actual, visible and available God's forgiveness of our sins. The positive power of our guilt is that it brings us to the Cross. Eugene O'Neill dramatised that truth in his powerful play, *Days Without End*, where two characters depict the two natures of John Loving. Two actors represent this split personality: John, the hopeful and eager searcher for truth and love; and Loving, wearing a mask whose features reproduce John's face with a sneer of scornful mockery. The drama rises to a climax when John, driven by guilt, stumbles into a church and staggers to the foot of the Cross where he had forsaken God in his youth. The sinister figure of Loving has followed him and tried to prevent his petition, but there at the Cross John wins his battle against his cynical self as the latter dies with these words, "Thou hast conquered, Lord! Thou art the end! Forgive the damned soul of John Loving!"[4]

The 130th Psalm pleads for a positive attitude to the emotion of guilt. Instead of being ashamed of it and regarding it as a sign of sickness, we are encouraged to regard it as a sign of moral health. Any experience, however miserable, contributes to our healing when it turns us to God, forces us to face our human frailty, compels us to examine our basic beliefs and puts us in a mood to receive God's forgiveness. God can do something with a person who says, "I wait for the Lord, my soul doth wait, and in his word do I hope . . ."

NOTES TO PSALM 130

1. Toronto *Globe and Mail*, 31 December, 1977.
2. Charles W. Colson, *Born Again* (Hodder and Stoughton, London, 1976)
3. Published by Hawthorn Books Inc., New York, 1973.
4. Eugene O'Neill, *Days Without End* (Random House, New York).

PSALM 138

He Feels Confident

"The Lord will accomplish his purpose for me."[1] That has to be one of the most daring statements of faith in the Bible. To believe in God at all, to believe that he is a living God, to believe that he has a purpose which includes each human life, and to believe that, no matter what happens, God's purpose will be accomplished—what a faith to live by!

Many people do not live by that faith. Some don't believe in a personal God at all. Their idea of God is that of the watchmaker who started the world's mechanism going, then withdrew to let it run down. Even those who hold the Biblical view of God, who see him not only as the Author of history but as being very much involved in history, cannot always fit the individual into the picture. They hope that God is working out a good purpose for the human race, taking his creation to some "far-off divine event", but they cannot believe that the great God is concerned with each human life in the way that a loving parent is concerned with each of his children. They think that God is too high and we are too lowly. Therefore it seems crass conceit to say, "The Lord will accomplish his purpose for me."

Yet the writer of the 138th Psalm says it. He declares specifically, "For the Lord, high as he is, cares for the lowly." This Hebrew poet knows what he is talking about because he is one of the lowly ones and God has cared for him. His confidence is really a reaction to God's loving care. He was in serious trouble that threatened to take his life. He asked God for help, and God answered with an act of deliverance which seemed to him more marvellous than all the mighty acts of God in history. He shouts his praise, makes it public, wants everyone to hear about it. He goes to the temple and sings a psalm of thanksgiving and summons the kings of the earth to join him. He believes that what God has done for him is a gospel for the whole world.

> *I will praise thee, O Lord, with all my heart;*
> *boldly, O God, will I sing psalms to thee.*
> *I will bow down towards thy holy temple,*
> *for thy love and faithfulness I will praise thy name;*
> *for thou hast made thy promise wide as the heavens.*
> *When I called to thee thou didst answer me*
> *and make me bold and valiant-hearted.*
> *Let all the kings of the earth praise thee, O Lord,*
> *when they hear the words thou hast spoken;*
> *and let them sing of the Lord's ways,*
> *for great is the glory of the Lord.*
> *For the Lord, high as he is, cares for the lowly . . .*

Now comes the daring statement of faith, *"The Lord will accomplish his purpose for me."* There is nothing academic about that faith. It is not the kind that you work out in a theological seminar by discussing the question, "Does God have a purpose for each human life?" The theological question does not come first. The experience of God comes first, and we respond to it with faith as the Psalmist did. God's saving activity in his life gave him confidence that God must have a purpose for him and that, no matter what happened, that purpose would be accomplished. That's a faith to live by. We *do* live by that faith, we can live by it, because it does three things in a person's life: it sustains, restrains and constrains.

"The Lord will accomplish his purpose for me." By such a faith I am *sustained in my defeats*. I do suffer defeats simply because I have purposes of my own. I must have them, or life would not be worth living. I want to pursue a useful career and be successful and do some good in the world and enjoy my home and family and one day retire in comfort. It's a modest purpose, yet many things can defeat it. My health may break down. My work may become too difficult. My job may cease to exist. People may spurn what I try to do for them. Tragedy may snatch away my loved ones. Then my world is shattered, my plans destroyed, my purposes defeated.

Suppose I believe that God has a purpose for me which is larger and wiser and better than my own? Then I am sustained in the confidence that the defeat of my purpose need not mean the defeat of God's purpose. At the very least I can look at life from the perspective of God who sees beyond my defeats to his victories. I am like a little girl who has broken her favourite doll and is dissolved in tears because her whole world has been shattered. Her father, with larger perspective, knows that there will be other dolls. He knows that this little tragedy will not be final if he can teach her how to manage it. So he puts his arms around the child, he loves her, he cries with her and weaves the broken doll into his larger purpose for her life.

There are many characters in the Bible who learned by experience that the defeat of their purposes did not mean the defeat of God's purpose. The Apostle Paul was always receiving direct messages to that effect. Here are three from the Book of Acts. In Corinth, when his enemies tried to silence him and drive him out of the city, the Lord said to him, "Have no fear: go on with your preaching and do not be silenced, for I am with you and no one shall attempt to do you harm; and there are many in this city who are my people." (18:9-10 NEB) In a Jerusalem prison, with a lynch-mob outside plotting his death, Paul heard the Lord say, "Keep up your courage; you have affirmed the truth about me in Jerusalem, and you must do the same in Rome." (23:11) On the voyage to Rome, when a terrible storm arose and threatened to smash the ship to pieces, Paul the prisoner in chains heard the voice of the Lord, "Do not be afraid, Paul . . . it is ordained that you shall appear before the Emperor; and, be assured, God has granted you the lives of all who are sailing with you!" (27:24) Again and again, when shipwreck, imprisonment, hostility, ill-health and failure frustrated his own purpose, Paul was sustained by the faith of the Psalmist, "The Lord will accomplish his purpose for me."

In that faith I may even see my defeat as a constructive element in God's purpose for me. Some years ago, when I was lecturing at a pastors' conference in the United States, a young Baptist minister told me about his personal situation. He said that he had resigned his church, that his wife had given up a good teaching position, and that they had invested all their resources in a specialised Christian ministry which was not working out as they had hoped. He felt frustrated and defeated. Almost in tears he said, "I have reached the conclusion that God is not in it." Perhaps that was true. On the other hand, God may have been very much in it. In this experience of apparent failure God may have been using the young couple as he could never have used them in success.

In his famous poem, "Rabbi ben Ezra" Robert Browning proposed a creative way of dealing with our defeats:

> Then, welcome each rebuff
> That turns earth's smoothness rough,
> Each sting that bids nor sit nor stand but go!
> Be our joys three-parts pain!
> Strive, and hold cheap the strain;
> Learn, nor account the pang; dare, never
>   grudge the throe!

I once knew of a man who "welcomed each rebuff". Whenever any kind of trouble blocked his path, he clasped it by the hand and said, "I welcome you as a messenger from the Great King. What are you saying to me? What are you trying to teach me? What do you contribute to my eternal self-discipline and to the ultimate usefulness of my life? How do you fit into God's good purpose?" That's a faith to live by because it sustains us in our defeats. "The Lord will accomplish his purpose for me."

By such a faith I am *restrained in my victories*. Life does have victories, thank God, and they taste sweet, especially when they are the fruit of long and difficult struggle. A man and wife, of modest means and little education, encourage their son to work his way through college. One day he graduates with honours and the promise of a useful career ahead of him. Another person borrows a few dollars and buys a small business and by sheer hard work puts it on its feet and expands it into a flourishing enterprise. We congratulate such people. They have won victories. They have a right to rejoice in the fulfilment of their dreams and purposes.

Suppose God also has a purpose for us? What difference

should that make in our victories? What difference to the
Psalmist? He had won a victory over trouble, and that's no
small accomplishment. The great victories in life are won not
on the battle-fields of military conflict, not in the sports arena,
not in the market-place or the scientific laboratory but in the
souls of men. They are the spiritual victories over illness,
sorrow, resentment, revenge and frustration. What did the
Psalmist do? He didn't bask in his own glory. Instead, he gave
the glory to God. He went to church and sang a psalm of praise,
and it was not conventional praise but a lifting up of his heart to
God for mercies which were recent and vivid. In his gratitude
he resolved to praise God for the rest of his life.

Other people react differently. They become self-sufficient in
their good health, success, money, prosperity and comfort.
Instead of binding them to God, their victories separate them
from God. Thus the affluent society becomes "the secular
society", a phrase we never heard when our nation was at war
or sunk in the misery of economic depression. It is now, when
people have money to spend and gadgets to play with and leisure
time in which to enjoy them, now in the flush of moral and economic victory that we hear talk about the "death of God" and
"man come of age" and "the post-Christian era". We have
become drunk in the accomplishment of our own purposes.

We should be more restrained in our self-congratulation if we
believed that God has a purpose for our lives. We should realise
that not we ourselves but God is the Author of all we possess
and that the God who gives is also the God who takes away.
We should realise also that God gives for a purpose, and it
cannot be a selfish purpose. Therefore, we shall stay close to
God in order to discover his purpose and make our victory
serve it.

That is the motive behind all that the Bible means by stewardship, the idea if not the word. Stewardship is the acceptance
of life as a trust from God, the acceptance of all our gifts,
abilities and material possessions as a means of serving God.
That was the motive behind Albert Schweitzer's amazing
career of Christian service. In his early years he distinguished
himself as a musician, theologian, philosopher and preacher.
He won significant victories in all those spheres. He was flushed
with success. Yet he was continually restrained by the question

which he asked himself, "What is God's purpose for me? What is the highest service in which I can use my varied gifts?" The answer to that question sent him to medical school and a lifetime of service as a missionary in French Equatorial Africa. Schweitzer believed in God's purpose, he lived by it and dedicated his life to its accomplishment, one of the most significant lives in the history of Christianity. Looking at him we can only say again, "What a faith to live by!"

"The Lord will accomplish his purpose for me." By such a faith I am *constrained in my obedience*. The word "constrained" is not a coercive word. When you say that you feel constrained to do something you don't mean that you are being forced to do it. Rather you feel a sense of obligation, an inner impulse, something tugging you in that direction.

Every loving relationship places constraint upon people. A youth decides to follow his father's advice in the choice of a career, not because his father compels him but because his father loves him and has a purpose for him and because he feels constrained by his father's loving purpose. The faith that God loves us and has a good purpose for our lives brings us under similar constraint. God is Infinite Wisdom, Infinite Love, Infinite Power. He sees the whole course of our life. Whatever way we take, he knows what the outcome will be. Not only so, but God is on our side, he wants what is best for us. Therefore, we are constrained to obey him, to consult him, to discover his purpose and bring our lives into harmony with it.

The 138th Psalm was one man's reaction to a saving experience of God. God came into his life and did for him what nobody else could do. The Authorised Version translates the opening verse, "I will praise thee with my whole heart: before the gods will I sing praise unto thee." Those ancient men of God could fall into the language of polytheism when they wanted to score the impotence of gods other than their own. Polytheism has not disappeared. People still create their own objects of worship, their little idols and give them the trust and loyalty and devotion that belong only to God. They worship houses and money and work and motor cars and children—all of which are good in themselves but are not meant to be worshipped because they are not powerful to save. They don't deliver us from defeat. They don't give us victory over our worst enemies. Only God can do that, God who will accomplish his purpose for us.

We have that confidence because we believe that he is the God and Father of our Lord Jesus Christ. He is the God who made himself known in Christ. He is the God who showed us in Christ our own life lived in perfect obedience to his purpose. There lies our constraint. Paul wrote about it in his Second Letter to the Corinthians when he said, "For the love of Christ constraineth us . . ." (5:14 AV) Love is always the great constrainer. Whatever is finest in our characters was not flogged into them but was drawn out by the sight of something good and loving and sacrificial to which we responded.

Rufus Jones, the Quaker philosopher, tells of a time in his childhood when he learned that lesson. He had flagrantly disobeyed his mother and expected to be punished severely. Instead, as he says, "a miracle happened". His mother led him to his room, sat him down on a chair, put her hands on his head and told God all about him. She interpreted her dreams for him. She portrayed the boy and the man of her hopes. She told God what she had always expected him to be and how he had disappointed her hope. "O God", she said, "take this boy of mine and make him the boy and man he is divinely designed to be." Then she bent over and kissed him and went out and left him alone in the silence with God.[2]

How does the human heart respond to such a gracious and loving constraint? We could fight a God who overawed us with his thunderbolts and frightened us with prophecies of punishment, but what are we going to do with the strange God who humbles himself and comes where we are and says to each one of us, "I have a great purpose for you, my child. I want you to live a life in my Kingdom, a life in friendship with me. But I shall not force you into it. I shall reveal this life before your eyes. I shall hold it up before you and let you see it in its highest and best. I shall constrain you with my love."? What shall we do with that God but obey him?

"The Lord will accomplish his purpose for me." That is a faith to live by, a faith that sustains us in our defeats, restrains us in our victories, constrains us in our obedience, a faith that is really our response to the saving love of God in Jesus Christ.

NOTES TO PSALM 138

1. The treatment of this Psalm follows the translation in the New English Bible.
2. Quoted in *The Interpreter's Bible*, Vol. 3 (Abingdon Press, Nashville, 1954) pp. 1029-1031.

Psalm 146

He Feels Trust

One of the most moving scenes in the Old Testament is the scene where Joseph makes himself known to his brothers. (Gen 45:1ff) Years earlier they sold him as a slave to a caravan of traders travelling to Egypt. Now in a time of famine they came to Egypt to buy food, never dreaming that the governor who interviewed them was their own brother. Joseph forgave them freely and fully. The ruling Pharaoh was so impressed with this generous gesture that he urged Joseph to send for his whole family and settle them in one of the lushest regions in the land. Unfortunately that Pharaoh did not live forever. He died and was succeeded by others, until there came to the throne one of whom we read, "Now there arose a new king over Egypt, who did not know Joseph." (Exodus 1:8 RSV) That king had a very different policy toward the aliens living in his land. He oppressed them, persecuted them and made them slaves.

Whatever else that bitter experience gave to God's ancient people, it must have given them a philosophy of life that was articulated centuries later by the writer of the 146th Psalm: *"Put not your trust in princes, nor in the son of man, in whom there is no help. His breath goeth forth, he returneth to his earth; in that very day his thoughts perish."* Trust people but not too much—that is the theme of the 146th Psalm.

On the surface it seems like a cynical theme and not too realistic. We have to trust people. All good community life depends upon it. We exercise trust every time we step on a pedestrian crossing, every time we board an aeroplane or eat in a restaurant or get a prescription filled at a drug store. We trust the surgeon who takes our life in his hands, the teacher who moulds our children's minds, the politician who takes our tax money and governs the country. Business depends on trust; where it is present we can buy and sell without fear. Family life can be happy only when husbands and wives, parents and children have confidence in one another. International treaties and the achievement of world peace depend on mutual trust. We really have no other choice. Trust is a natural and necessary response to life; without it we could not survive.

The writer of the 146th Psalm does not dispute that. He knows that we have to trust people but at the same time he insists that we ought not to trust them too much. There is a limit beyond which trust becomes unreasonable expectation and lays upon people a burden which they are not able to bear. It's like driving across a bridge. For years the bridge stands strong, carrying a normal load of traffic, but vehicles multiply and get bigger, and one day under a high wind too many bunch together on the bridge, and it collapses. The bridge itself is not defective; it simply wasn't built to carry such a heavy load. Such is the human spirit which breaks under too heavy a load of trust. That is why the Psalmist says, in effect, trust people but not too much.

It is important to emphasise that he is not being cynical. Nothing in the 146th Psalm indicates that the author had a low view of his fellow-men. If he doesn't trust people, it's not because they are deficient in character but because they are human, frail and fallible, they collapse like the bridge. Eventually they grow old and die and can therefore guarantee no permanency to their plans and purposes. In that very day their thoughts perish.

To their sorrow the descendants of Joseph discovered that truth. They trusted the king, but the king died. He returned to the dust, and all their hopes went into the dust with him. The Psalmist may have suffered a similar experience. In a personal crisis he may have counted on the support of a loyal friend who had stood by him all through his life but, when he went for help, he found that his friend, whom he hadn't seen for a while, had become old and senile and incapable of helping him. It is the experience of a faithful employee whose boss puts his hand on his shoulder and says, "As long as I am alive you've got a job with this company." The employee might well ask, "How long do you expect to stay alive?" One day the boss suffers a fatal heart attack, there is a reshuffling of the power structure, and the axe falls. "His breath goeth forth, he returneth to his earth; in that very day his thoughts perish."

Or the Psalmist may have been thinking of some national crisis. His situation may have been like that of the prophet Isaiah who grew up during the long and prosperous reign of King Uzziah, probably the greatest king in Palestine since Solomon. The people's admiration invested him with all the qualities of ideal monarchy. He represented security to them. They trusted him and thought he would live forever. To their dismay, however, he contracted leprosy, and his leprosy was seen as the judgment of God upon a sin in which the whole nation was involved. It must have been shattering for the young Isaiah to realise that, although Uzziah had been a good king, he was mortal and fallible and the people had been mistaken to place in him such absolute trust. If the 146th Psalm had been written at that time, Isaiah could well have quoted it.

We are looking at the ultimate failure of humanism. The humanist believes that man, having mastered his physical environment, should be able, without any help from outside, to solve his basically moral problems and make this earth a paradise. Yet the weakness of that argument is that moral accomplishments are not always carried over from one generation to another. A single generation can dissipate, exhaust or destroy the moral legacy of centuries. We have seen that happen in more than one country during our lifetime. To be sure, idealists can lift the human race to high levels but they can guarantee no permanency to their plans and purposes. "In that very day his thoughts perish." That does turn people into cynics, as it turned H. G. Wells into a cynic. In his early years he rejoiced in the godlike capacities of man but in his last book, *Mind at the End of its Tether*, he wrote,

> The human story has already come to an end . . . and homo sapiens in his present form is played out. The stars in their courses have turned against him, and he has to give place to some other animal better adapted to face the fate that closes in more swiftly upon

mankind . . . Our universe is not merely bankrupt;
there remains no dividend at all; it is not simply
liquidated; it is going clean out of existence.[1]

There is no such despair in the 146th Psalm. Its author is not
saying that we mustn't expect anything of our fellow-men but
rather that we must not expect too much of them. To give them
absolute trust is to ask the impossible and therefore to experience a crisis of confidence. Civilised life demands that we trust
one another; but we shall find a broken reed if we lean on our
neighbours as we can lean only upon God. *That* is the positive
thrust of the 146th Psalm. The author wants not to discourage
faith in people but to encourage faith in God. After counselling
us not to put our trust in earthly rulers he says, "*Happy is he that
hath the God of Jacob for his help, whose hope is in the Lord his God.*" In
that affirmation he responds to his own experience of the grace
and goodness of God. He believes that while there is a limit to
trust in man, there is no limit to trust in God. We can trust God
implicitly, absolutely and eternally.

The Psalmist believes that we can trust God because he has
resources of power that man does not have. That is still true.
Although modern man does have power undreamed of by past
generations, there are still many things he has not done and
cannot do. He cannot create a whale — which was an awesome
sight to a character in a novel, a nineteenth-century sea captain
who said that he was not a religious man but he could never
doubt God once he had clapped eyes on a whale. Man can build
a submarine that looks like a whale, but not a whale itself or the
ocean in which it swims. He can make satellites that cruise
among the stars, but not the stars themselves or the sun or the
moon. He can build jet aeroplanes that streak across the sky but
he cannot create the sky or the earth. Man himself is a creature,
and when we place ultimate trust in him we are trusting the
creature and not the Creator — which, according to Paul in his
Letter to the Romans (1:23), is a form of idolatry and corrup-
tion.

The Psalmist believes that God is powerful because he is the
Creator "*which made heaven, and earth, the sea, and all that therein
is . . .*" Like all the Hebrew poets he is obsessed with the

doctrine of Creation. He looks at the world about him and infers that the God who created such a marvellous world must be a marvellous God whose power can be trusted. Consider that power, as did one writer who said that if he had been present at the birth of this planet, and some archangel had turned to tell him that the blazing mass he was watching was on its way to cool and become the cradle of cultures and civilisations, he would have listened respectfully but would have determined never to talk with such a demented, deranged angel again. Creation is rather incredible when you look at it through a telescope or a microscope or with the naked eye. No wonder some of the great scientists have classed themselves among the ranks of devoutly religious men. Creation spoke to them, as it spoke to the Psalmist, of the power of the Creator, a power we can trust.

The Psalmist believed also that we can trust God because he has used his limitless power to care for his children. I got a glimpse of God's loving, personal care on the one occasion when I was privileged to watch an open-heart operation. The patient lying on the table was a six-year-old girl. Looking down from the balcony at the surgeons, doctors, nurses, machines, equipment and instruments that surrounded her, I suddenly realised that the concentrated medical knowledge and skill of the centuries was now focussed on that one little child and I thought to myself, "The love of God is like that." Sometimes all heaven's energies are focussed on one helpless person, and God is saying, "Let my universe run itself while I attend to the needs of my child."

That's what overawed the Psalmist. He praised not only God's majesty and splendour and dominion and power in Creation but God's concern for the hungry, the oppressed, the friendless, the blind, the widow and the orphan. Perhaps he himself belonged to one of those classes, and perhaps God did for him what others whom he trusted were unable to do. He saw that the glory of God resides in his goodness—a discovery that Moses made when he said to God, "I pray thee, show me thy glory," and God replied, "I will make all my goodness pass before you." (Exodus 33:18 RSV) All of God's goodness passed before the Psalmist. He praised the God *"which executeth judgment for the oppressed: which giveth food to the hungry"*. He sang a hymn of praise: *"The Lord looseth the prisoners: the Lord openeth the eyes of the blind: the Lord raiseth them that are bowed down: the Lord loveth the righteous: the Lord preserveth the strangers: he relieveth the fatherless and widow: but the way of the wicked he turneth upside down."*

One of the great Chinese Christian leaders in modern times, T. Z. Koo, used to tell of an experience which proved to him that to God alone belongs ultimate trust. He said that when the Japanese sent their planes in wave after wave over China, he and others had to go out into the fields because they had no dugouts in the city. When the final air raid warning sounded, they knew that in ten minutes the planes would arrive. Dr. Koo said that in that short ten minutes he lived through the experiences of a lifetime. A feeling of utter helplessness swept over him. The usual things with which they surrounded their lives suddenly lost their significance. Most of them had been thinking that if they had money in the bank they would be fairly secure; but as he sat there waiting he realised that no amount of money, not even of American dollars, could be of any help to him. He used to pride himself in the fact that he was a university graduate, but what could a Ph.D. do for him as he sat there waiting for the planes? One after another all those things fell away, until he saw that there under the sky in the fields he was before his Maker just as he was, stripped of everything, nothing more to fall back on. And his lips began to whisper, "Yea, though I walk in the shadow of death, I will fear no evil, for thou art with me." That was no doctrine then. It was no precept in a code of ethics. It was not a beautiful phrase in a poem. It meant that he was not alone, that he had found something in life which no disaster could wipe out.

The Psalmist had another reason for trusting God. He believed that God is sovereign and that his sovereignty never ends. *"The Lord shall reign for ever, even thy God, O Zion, unto all generations."* The tragedy of the Hebrews in Egypt was that an earthly king did not reign forever. He died and was succeeded by another king with a policy that differed drastically from that of his predecessors. Suppose the universe were governed by a succession of gods, such as the Greeks worshipped on Mount Olympus, each with a different policy, one benevolent, another despotic, another indifferent. Suppose God himself were limited and finite and could be defeated and deposed.

The Psalmist celebrates the conviction that God is infinite and cannot be deposed. He believed that as long as the universe endures, and long afterwards, the heart of Reality will be caring love, the love that embraced him and would embrace his children and children's children to all generations. That affirmation of faith was his response to his experience of God in history. Like all Hebrews he saw history as a Divine drama in which God by a succession of mighty acts had established his sovereignty again and again. Earthly kings might come and go, but the Lord shall reign forever. Therefore he is worthy to be trusted.

Only God is worthy of ultimate trust because only God is great. That was the conviction of the French preacher who spoke at the funeral service of King Louis XIV in Notre Dame. The cathedral was gorgeously decorated that day. Beauty, social distinction, high rank and political power had crowded into it. The pomp and circumstance of a proud and glittering age had met to honour the king who had been a symbol of the times. Sophisticated, "superior" men and women sat back to listen to the eulogy that the preacher was expected to utter, but the preacher's words fell with an icy chill. "Only God is great," he said. That was true and it has always been true. Earthly kings come and go, but the Lord shall reign forever.

Trust people but not too much. Yet there is a Person, One above all others whom we may trust absolutely. He is Jesus Christ, the God-Man in whom dwelt all the fullness of the eternal God. He is the co-Creator of whom the Fourth Gospel declares, "all things were made through him, and without him was not anything made that was made." (John 1:3 RSV) He demonstrated the power of God over nature, disease, evil and death. He made visible the care of God for the hungry, the oppressed, the friendless, the blind, the widow and the orphan. He is sovereign, for in raising Christ from the dead and exalting him to glory God has made him Lord of time and eternity. We can trust him forever.

Not only trust but praise him with such unending praise as the Psalmist commanded from his own soul. He resolved to devote the remainder of his earthly life to the praise of God.

"While I live will I praise the Lord: I will sing praises unto my God while I have any being." The Gospel promises that we shall have "being" even beyond death. In that hope we shall trust God and praise him not only in this life but through all eternity.

NOTES TO PSALM 146

1. Published by William Heinemann Ltd., 1945.